Getting into
America

Books to change your life and work.
Accessible, easy to read and easy to act on –
other titles in the **How To** series include:

Teaching Abroad
How and where to find teaching and lecturing jobs worldwide

Living & Working in America
The complete guide to a successful short or long-term stay

Getting a Job in America
Working in the USA – a step-by-step guide

Getting a Job Abroad
The handbook for the international jobseeker: where the jobs are, how to get them

Finding Voluntary Work Abroad
All the information you need for getting valuable work experience overseas

Send for a free copy of the latest catalogue to:
How To Books
3 Newtec Place,
Magdalen Road,
Oxford OX4 1RE,
United Kingdom
info@howtobooks.co.uk
http:/www/howtobooks.co.uk

Getting into
America

*The immigration guide to finding
a new life in the USA*

HENRY G. LIEBMAN
2nd edition

howtobooks

First published by How To Books Ltd,
3 Newtec Place, Magdalen Road,
Oxford OX4 1RE. United Kingdom.
Tel: (01865) 793806. Fax: (01865) 248780.
email: info@howtobooks.co.uk
www.howtobooks.co.uk

First published 1999
Second edition 2002

British Library Cataloguing in Publication Data
A catalogue record for this book is available from
the British Library

Cover design by Baseline Arts Ltd., Oxford

Produced for How To Books by Deer Park Productions
Typeset by Anneset, Weston-super-Mare, Somerset
Printed and bound by Cromwell Press, Trowbridge, Wiltshire

NOTE: The material contained in this book is set
out in good faith for general guidance and no
liability can be accepted for loss or expense
incurred as a result of relying in particular
circumstances on statements made in the book.
The laws and regulations are complex and liable
to change, and readers should check the current
position with the relevant authorities before
making personal arrangements.

Contents

About the Author

Henry Liebman is a 50-year-old attorney living and practising law in Seattle, Washington. After serving as a tax specialist for Touche Ross and Company, he became an associate for Franklin and Watkins Attorneys at Law and a member of the Board of Directors of Northwest International Bank. He then joined Franco, Asia, Bensussen. Henry Liebman is now managing partner in Liebman-Mimbu, PLLC, Attorneys at Law. He travels extensively to Asia and Europe in conjunction with his legal practice. He has two children, Rachel and Catherine, and his recreational pursuits include golf, hiking, mountain-climbing and world-wide travel.

LEGAL ASSISTANCE

There are many law firms able to help with your immigration needs. The author's Seattle-based firm, Liebman-Mimbu, PLLC, was first established in 1904, and provides legal services to an international clientele. One of the founders, Albert M. Franco, who has practised law since 1940, led the US Army G-2 in Kobe, Japan, immediately following World War II, and served as a consultant to the US Agency for International Development in Central and Latin Americas. Two members of the firm have served as Legislative Assistants to the US House of Representatives. Firm partner and author, Henry G. Liebman, concentrates on international legal matters and manages the firm's international and immigration law practice. He is the Business Immigration Ombudsman for PACE, a tri-lateral trade council for owners and managers of small- and mid-sized companies in Canada, the US and Mexico.

Main office
Liebman-Mimbu, PLLC, Attorneys at Law
3223 3rd Avenue South, Suite 200
Seattle, WA 98134
Tel: (206) 381 3775
Fax: (206) 381 3376
email: henry@usa-immigration.com
www: usa-immigration.com-homepage

Preface

The United States and Canada accept more immigrants
today than since the early 1900s. Several million tourists,
temporary workers, asylum seekers, refugees and permanent residents come to North America each year.
America's 'melting pot' and Canada's 'mosaic', once
almost entirely European, now include people from every
corner of the planet. People move to North America for
freedom, safety and opportunity, while appreciating the
unique blend of living space, political stability and high
standard of living.

North America is relatively open to immigrants.
However, as the continent fills with new arrivals, the doors
will slowly close. During the first 150 years of its history
the US accepted whoever arrived. Since the 1920s,
American immigration laws have regulated and prioritised
the flow of immigrants. Immigrating to the US now
requires foreigners seeking entry to position themselves in
the most advantageous immigrant categories.

SIMPLIFYING A COMPLEX SUBJECT

After practising immigration law for 22 years, I have
found that most clients pose the same questions.
Businessmen needing to bring critical personnel to the US
typically ask: 'How do I get my workers into the US?
How long does it take? And how much will it cost?'
Almost everyone wants to know, 'How do I get a green
card?'

Mere regurgitation of US immigration laws confuses
clients. Most people want to know the steps required to

immigrate, their options, how long the process takes, and their chances for success. They want the information presented in a simple, logical way. This book simplifies the complex subject in a way which I hope you'll find understandable and accessible.

It discusses immigration strategies for most scenarios. There are many confusing paths leading to a green card – the nonimmigrant visa list starts at 'A' and ends at 'S'. The list includes diplomats, vessel crew members, UN officials, NATO generals and staff, religious workers, as well as the more commonly used working visas. This book concisely points out the obstacles often encountered with an immigration scenario, and provides solutions.

- It explains how to obtain the best visa for your purposes – for work, investment, study in universities, or permanent residence.

- It teaches you how to interact with Immigration and Naturalization Service (INS) inspectors at border crossings and airports.

- It provides pointers for effective communication with consular officers when applying for visas abroad.

- It provides citizenship questions and answers for those who wish to complete the immigration process.

After reading this book, you'll be able to choose the best immigration strategy to accomplish your ultimate goal. You may be confident enough to handle your own case, or be able to tell your lawyer what you hope to accomplish.

Henry G. Liebman

1

The History of US Immigration

For all practical purposes, the US had open borders until
1875. Many states actually promoted immigration as the
US needed settlers to tame the North American
wilderness, and most of the new arrivals came from
Northern Europe.

The first serious attempts to limit immigration occurred
through a series of laws enacted between 1875 and 1917.
These laws excluded lunatics, convicts, all Chinese peoples,
beggars, anarchists, and carriers of contagious diseases.
Immigrants during this period were assessed a 50-cents-
per-person tax.

At the onset of the 20th century, the US received
upwards of one million immigrants per year. Most of the
new arrivals came from Eastern and Southern Europe,
and tended to be Roman Catholic, Eastern Orthodox or
Jewish, instead of belonging to America's predominant
religion at that time, Protestant Christianity. Many
newcomers couldn't read or speak English.

THE FIRST ATTEMPTS AT LIMITING IMMIGRANTS

A series of laws enacted between 1917 and 1924
attempted to limit the number of new immigrants. These
laws expanded the categories of excludable aliens,
established the **quota system**, and banned all Asians
except Japanese, who had made a 'gentleman's agreement'
with the US.

The quota system restricted the number of **visas** made
available to particular nationalities. The system, which
allocated visas according to the number of persons of the
same nationality living in the US, favoured the majority

ethnic groups, namely the Northern Europeans. The quota system limited the total visas issued to 150,000 per year, with no restrictions on persons born in the Western Hemisphere. Additionally, the US Congress decided to bar citizenship to 'Orientals', which meant that Asians, including Japanese, could no longer become US citizens.

By 1924, US immigration law limited the total number of aliens and imposed qualitative restrictions.

UNDERSTANDING THE MODERN IMMIGRATION SYSTEM

The next major change in immigration law occurred with the 1952 Act, which established the modern immigration system. The new quota system created limits on a per-country basis without regard to the number of persons of particular nationalities currently living in the US. Asian immigration was limited, rather than restricted.

The 1952 Act also established the **preference system** that gave priority to family members and people with special skills. This was the first attempt to target immigrants with special skills.

Subsequent changes to the immigration laws were driven by a more enlightened attitude toward civil rights. Positive changes were also due to the increasing need for US multinational corporations to attract skilled labour, and to transfer key personnel between the US and foreign operations.

In 1968 Congress officially abolished restrictions on Asian immigration. It also eliminated immigration discrimination based on race, place of birth, sex and residence. In 1970 Congress implemented the L-1 – or managerial-transfer – program. In 1976 Congress eliminated preferential treatment for residents of the Western Hemisphere.

TAKING NEW STEPS TO CURTAIL 'ILLEGALS'

By 1986 the US was facing the biggest immigration wave since the turn of the century. Only this time the majority of immigrants were from Latin America and Asia. The West Coast of the US and the border states with Mexico and Cuba received the brunt of these new arrivals. By some estimates, the number of 'illegals' exceeded the number of legal immigrants.

In 1986 changes to the immigration laws were intended to tighten up the system. Congress legalised hundreds of thousands of illegal immigrants, while introducing the employer-sanctions program which fines employers for hiring illegal workers. To curtail an epidemic of bogus marriages to US citizens, Congress passed tough laws to prevent marriage fraud.

Current limitations

While the 1986 Act focused on curtailing illegal immigration, the 1990 Act was aimed at helping US businesses attract skilled foreign workers. The 1990 Act established an annual limit of 675,000 permanent resident visas; 465,000 for family class; 140,000 for employment-based categories; and 55,000 for the visa lottery. On top of these limits, the law permits 125,000 refugees and smaller groups authorised by prior laws.

The 1990 Act also increased the number of employment-based visas from approximately 54,000 annually to 140,000 a year. The expanded business-class categories favour persons who make educational, professional, or financial contributions. For example, the 1990 Act created the Immigrant Investor Program. Conversely, the 1990 Act limited the number of non-immigrant visas available to professional workers to 65,000 per year. So far, most of the quota or numerical limitations of the 1990 Act for non-immigrant visas have not been reached.

A TREND TOWARDS MORE RESTRICTIONS

Today, the national debate has shifted to restricting immigration. Almost every national magazine and newspaper has run feature articles implying that immigrants take jobs from Americans. There are serious discussions on the negative effects immigration has on social services. The state of California passed a law that denies welfare benefits to illegals. Many politicians believe America needs a 'rest' from immigration, saying time is needed to absorb the millions of immigrants recently allowed into the country. Still other politicians want to liberalise employment- and investor-based immigration. The events of 11 September 2001 do nothing to stregthen the hand of the moderates.

The US Congress has been considering legislation that may restrict family-class and employment-based categories while increasing experience requirements for professional workers.

FORECASTING WHAT THE FUTURE HOLDS

I converse with the US Senate Sub Committee on Immigration on an occasional basis. I understand that the Senate will entertain proposals to overhaul the US immigration system. Proposals may include merging the **Immigration and Naturalization Service (INS)** with the Department of Labor, separating enforcement from visa petition processing, and further restrictions on employer-based immigration.

I predict Congress will try to balance the number of newcomers the country can absorb with the rights of families to reunify, the needs of businesses to attract the best workers in the world, and the need to attract foreign capital. The next few years will see attempts to tighten up the system and lessen the impact on American social services. On the other hand, the growing internationalism of US business will work to maintain or increase current levels of employment-based immigration.

Overall, we can expect continued pressure to reduce the numbers of immigrants, while at the same time improving the quality of their skills. Family class categories may be limited to immediate family members, while higher educational and/or experience requirements may be imposed on professional workers. There may be more encouragement for foreign investors.

The beauty of American immigration law is that the US has moved from an ethnically biased system which favoured Northern Europeans to one that is truly multinational, and allows freedom and opportunity for all. The US offers the only immigration policy in the world that is blind to race, religion, creed and colour. It's truly a unique social experiment which continues to evolve.

2

Understanding the Background and Basics of Visas

WHAT IS A VISA?

A visa – usually stamped in a passport – permits the bearer to apply for entry into a country. The US requires visas, unless a country qualifies for a **visa waiver**. Most European countries, and Japan, qualify for visa waivers. A visa waiver eliminates the visa requirement for business and pleasure trips under 90 days in duration.

Those who plan to work in the US need a visa regardless of how long they intend to remain in the county.

Foreigners living in the US for indefinite periods need a **green card**, or **permanent residence visa**.

TWO CATEGORIES OF VISAS

Visas are either **nonimmigrant**, *ie* temporary, or **immigrant**, *ie* permanent. Refer to the Glossary for a list of the visa categories and the appropriate chapters for full details.

Nonimmigrant visas

The holder of a nonimmigrant visa agrees to leave the US prior to the end of a permitted stay period. The US issues over 30 types of nonimmigrant visas designated by letters of the alphabet. The nonimmigrant visa holder may only engage in the approved activity or work for the petitioning employer. Validity periods vary with the type of nonimmigrant.

Immigrant visas

An immigrant visa permits the holder to live in the US for as long as the US is the permanent place of residence. Immigrant visa holders may engage in any activity and work for any employer without restrictions. The INS issues immigrant visa holders with an **Alien Registration Card** as evidence of permanent residence status. The card, now pinkish-blue, was originally green, hence its name the green card.

Green card holders enjoy all the rights and obligations of citizens except that they cannot vote, and are ineligible to receive some welfare benefits. Green card holders may apply for citizenship after the passage of three years for spouses of US citizens and five years for all other green card holders. Green card holders must file US income tax returns and, in the case of war, serve in the US armed forces if called to duty.

Who processes visas?

Overseas, foreign service officers and US consular posts issue all visas; you must obtain your first visa from a consular officer outside the US. These consuls work for the **Department of State**, an agency of the federal government that controls foreign affairs. Each US consular post determines its own filing procedures, and not all consular posts process visas. Ask the consular post nearest your home for its procedures before applying.

Most visa categories require INS approval of a visa petition, or before application at the consulate for a visa stamp. The INS, which is part of the Department of Justice, approves visa petitions but cannot issue visas.

Not every visa category requires INS pre-approval. Exceptions include:

- B-1/B-2 Temporary Business or Tourist Visas
- E-1/2 Treaty Trader/Investor
- I Information Media
- R Religious Workers

- And select categories pertaining to diplomats, military personnel and special cases.

INS pre-approval

In order to obtain INS visa approval, file your petition and supporting documents by mail or courier with one of the INS Regional Processing Centers in Vermont, Texas, Nebraska or California. (See Appendices for addresses.) The INS will render its decision by mail. There is nobody to talk to about your petition. The entire process is done in writing. If INS approves your petition, take the approval notice (Form I-797), Consular Visa Application (Form OF-156) and your passport to the US consulate in your area to apply for the visa.

Consular processing

Consuls decide who receives a visa. The consul may accept an INS pre-approval, or the officer may ask you for more information, conduct an interview, or deny your visa application. The consul may deny your visa application even though the INS approved the petition. Normally the consul will issue the visa petition according to the INS approval. Upon approval the consul places the visa stamp in your passport. The stamp shows the place and date of issue, the number of permitted entries, duration, visa type and if applicable, the name of the US employer.

UNDERSTANDING HOW THE INS AND CONSULS EVALUATE VISA PETITIONS

The INS adjudicates visa petitions solely upon the information contained in the forms, the cover letter and supporting documents. The INS makes no personal contact with the applicant. The consulate bases its decision upon the same criteria, except that it may request a personal interview. As a rule, consulates request interviews only when they suspect a problem. Both INS and consular applications require detailed documentation.

GETTING THE GREEN LIGHT TO ENTER

Once you have your visa you may apply for entry to the US. The INS controls who enters the US just as the consuls control who receives visas. The INS may deny your entry to the US even if you have a valid visa.

If the INS admits you into the US it will stamp your **Arrival Departure Card** (Form I-94) with the date of entry, visa type and expiration date. The I-94 card issued by the INS determines how long you may stay in the US. Airline flight attendants distribute I-94 cards before landing at an international airport.

FORM I-94 AND VISA EXPIRATION DATES

The **expiration dates** on the I-94 card and your visa may differ. The I-94 expiration date determines how long you may stay in the US, while the visa merely indicates the time period during which you may apply for entry. For example, a **multiple entry visa**, valid for three years, permits unlimited applications to enter the US during the three-year visa validity period.

You must leave the US or extend your I-94 by the I-94 expiration date even if your visa is valid beyond that period. For example, you have a three-year visa but the INS only admits you for two years. In other words, the I-94 form expires before the visa does. In this case you must leave the US, or extend your I-94 form, prior to the I-94 expiration date even though you have a valid visa.

Overstaying expiration dates

Failure to leave the US on or before the I-94 expiration date results in the automatic cancellation of your visa. Because the US does not have a reliable system for matching entrance and exit dates, INS inspectors allow 48 hours from the I-94 expiration date to enter another country. If your passport does not contain a timely entry stamp, or another proof of entry to another country, you may be denied entry to the US. Because many countries do not routinely stamp passports, those who wish to return to the US on the same visa should make sure their passports are stamped or retain the airline tickets.

Overstays must apply for a new visa in their home country. To further complicate matters, consuls generally deny visas to persons who overstayed without a compelling reason. Compelling reasons include cancelled airline flights, sickness, death and emergencies.

People who overstay for six months up to one year may not re-enter the US for three years. Those who overstay for one year or more may not re-enter the US for ten years. Exceptions are made in cases of family emergency or extreme hardship to separated family members.

BEING DENIED ENTRY: YOUR OPTIONS

Summary removal procedures give the INS the right to deny entry to anybody they feel is misrepresenting the purpose of their stay in the US, such as persons holding tourist visas intending to work or to marry in the US. There is no right to a hearing or appeal and the applicant for entry may be barred from coming to the US for five years.

The INS may, in its sole discretion, merely exclude an applicant from entering the US without summary removal. This means the applicant for entry is sent home on the next flight but is not barred from further entry to the US. Alternatively, the INS may allow the applicant the right to a hearing.

The summary removal proceedings were designed to deter people who enter as tourists and illegally work, study or even marry in the US. Innocent people tend to be victimised by summary removal proceedings when they make inconsistent statements, act nervously and are generally not sure of themselves.

I often find that the visa applicant lied when the truth would have worked. Don't try to be an expert, don't try to anticipate what the inspector or consular officer wants to hear. Just calmly tell the truth and you will find that you

will have fewer problems at the airport and that
government officials will be helpful. You will also save
money on lawyers' fees.

CHANGE OF STATUS AND EXTENSION OF STAY

Once admitted to the US, a change in plans or
employment may require an **extension of stay** or **change
in visa status**. Provided that you did not violate the terms
of your stay, you may extend the I-94 form or change
immigration status while in the US. Applications for
extensions or changes of status must be made through one
of the INS Regional Processing Centers by filing
appropriate forms and supporting documents. The INS
must receive such petitions on or before the I-94
expiration date. Other than in exceptional circumstances,
the INS denies I-94 extensions that are filed late. You may
remain in the US during the process, even if the
processing period extends beyond the I-94 validity date.

You may remain in the US if you extend your I-94 or
change status on or before the I-94 expiration date. You
may remain in the US for 120 days after the I-94
expiration date to wait for the INS response to your
request for change of status or extension. Normally, 120
days suffice for INS processing. If the INS fails to respond
during the 120-day period, you may request an extension
of the 120-day period.

Extensions require proof that you intend to stay in the
US in the same employment capacity, and you must
explain why you need the extension. The INS treats
changes from one nonimmigrant status to another
nonimmigrant status as a new petition. INS approval of an
extension or change of status only permits you to remain
in the US; you need a valid visa if you leave and wish to
re-enter the country.

VISA REVALIDATION

You may revalidate an expired visa while in the US. The Visa Office in Washington, DC only accepts mailed applications for visa revalidation. In addition to the documentation required for any petition, applicants must prove that they have a valid I-94 card at the time of application. Those who don't qualify for revalidation must apply for their visa abroad.

The Visa Office provides a convenient alternative to travelling abroad for visa holders who qualify for revalidation, but it only revalidates the same visa category. For example, a person with an expired L-1A visa may apply for another L-1A visa through the Visa Office. A person changing from L-1A to E-1 may not apply for revalidation.

NORTH AMERICAN FREE TRADE ACT VISAS

Canadians are visa-exempt except for **treaty trader** and **treaty investor** visas which are controlled by a different treaty from NAFTA. Canadians must file for treaty trader or treaty investor visas at the US Consulate in Toronto. Canadians must use the treaty trader or treaty investor visa stamp to enter the US in that capacity.

Canadian tourists or business visitors do not need a visa or prior INS approval to enter the US. In most other cases, such as managers, professionals and treaty nationals whose occupations are on the skills list, Canadians merely present the INS approval letter at the border crossing. The INS inspector will issue an I-94 to evidence the correct status and stay period. No visa is required.

Canadians are supposed to be able to file and receive one-day adjudication of visa petitions at border posts. In reality the system does not work. Most border posts merely forward the visa petitions to a regional INS processing centre.

SUMMARY

- A visa allows you to apply for entry to the US.

- Only the consuls issue visas.

- A single entry visa allows you to apply for entry one time within the visa validity period.

- A multiple entry permits you to apply for entry unlimited times within the visa validity period.

- You are applying for admission to the US when you show your passport to the INS inspector at the airport or port of entry.

- The INS determines who comes into the USA and the length of stay.

- The I-94 card is evidence of how long you may stay in the US.

- Once you are inside the US, if you maintain legal status you may extend your stay or change to another visa status.

- If you leave the US you must have a valid visa to re-enter.

- Tell the truth to consuls and immigration inspectors and you will avoid summary removal proceedings. It's always better to tell the truth and return home rather than be barred from entry for five years.

BASIC CONCEPTS OF NONIMMIGRANT VISAS

The law creates two general types of visas: nonimmigrant and immigrant. A nonimmigrant visa terminates at a certain date. The immigrant visa holder may stay in the USA as long as he or she makes the US their permanent residence.

- With the exception of visa waiver countries, you need a

visa in order to enter the United States for business or pleasure trips. If you plan to work in the US you need a visa regardless of how long you intend to remain. Visa waiver permits nationals of certain countries to enter the US for 90 days or less for business or tourist reasons. Most European countries and Japan qualify.

- The United States consulate or embassy located abroad issues all visas. INS may approve visa petitions, or requests for a visa, but INS does not issue visas. In most cases applicants must first obtain INS approval and then apply for a visa from the consulate. Consulates may approve and issue B-1/B-2, E-1/2, I, R and a few other categories.

- To obtain INS visa approval file your petition with INS in the USA. Most petitions must be filed by mail or courier at one of four Regional Processing Centers. See Appendix 3.

- The INS will mail its decision as you instruct on the forms. If INS approves your petition, take the approval notice, Form I-797, Form OF-156 (consular visa application form) and your passport to the US consulate that serves your area to apply for the visa. You must obtain your initial visa outside the US.

- The consul may accept the INS decision, ask you for more information, interview you, or deny your visa application. The consuls have complete control over who receives visas. The consul may deny your visa application even if INS approved your petition. Normally the consul will issue visas according to the INS approval. The Consul places the visa stamp in your passport. The stamp shows place of issue, date of issue, number of permitted entries, duration, visa type, and if applicable the name of the US employer.

- Once you have your visa you may apply for entry to the US. INS controls who enters the US just as the consuls control who receives visas. INS may deny your entry to the US even if you have a valid visa. For example, if the INS inspector thinks a student is not really in school, he may deny entry. Often business cards to not match the employer noted under the visa stamp. The INS inspector may suspect you work for a different company from the one that applied for the visa. In such a case you may be denied entry.

- If INS admits you to the US they will stamp Form I-94 Arrival Departure Card with the date of entry, visa type and expiration date. The airplane crew hand out I-94 cards before landing. The dates on the I-94 card determine how long you may stay in the US.

- The dates on the I-94 card may be different from the dates on the visa. The I-94 card is evidence of how long you may stay in the US. You must leave the US or extend your I-94 by the I-94 expiration date, even if your visa is valid.

- With one exception, if the INS denies entry to the US you may either take the next flight home or ask for a hearing before an Immigration Judge. If you come to the US on visa waiver and INS denies entry for any reason, you must return. You have no right to a trial if you use visa waiver.

- It's always best to tell the truth to the consuls and to the Immigration Inspectors. If you tell the truth, they often try to help you. Most problems can be solved. If you lie nobody can help you. You can be barred from coming to the US for life if the consul or INS Inspector believes you committed fraud or materially misrepresented facts. Often, the truth would have worked. Don't try to be an expert, to anticipate what the Inspector or consular officer wants to hear. Calmly tell the truth and you will have fewer problems at the airport and government officials will be helpful. You will also save money on lawyers' fees.

3

Using a B-1 Visa

The **B-1 visa** permits business trips of less than six months' duration. The B-1 business visitor may not be employed in the US and must be paid from abroad. Because a visa waiver, if available, permits the same activities as the B-1, the B-1 visa is most often used for ongoing business, scientific or professional collaboration that takes more than 90 days to complete. Permissible activities include:

- business meetings
- scientific collaboration
- inspection of business opportunities
- meetings with government officials
- purchase of products
- negotiation of contracts
- selling products or services
- certain warranty or repair work.

With one exception B-1 visa holders may not work in the US. Foreign technicians may make warranty and repair service calls on B-1 visas within one year after the sale of the product, pursuant to a written purchase contract between the buyer and seller promising warranty and repair services.

APPLYING FOR ENTRY ON A B-1 VISA

To avoid problems at a port of entry B-1 visa holders should present documents that prove the purpose of their trip. Effective documentation may include:

- a copy of the warranty and repair contract if applicable
- an explanatory letter from the employer abroad
- a letter of invitation from the US business contacts
- a detailed itinerary.

You may also want to have somebody meet you at the airport to further explain the purpose of your trip or for language assistance.

WHAT CONSTITUTES WORK?

The primary purpose of the Immigration and Nationality Act is to protect US workers from cheap foreign labour. B-1 visa holders have the burden of convincing the INS inspector that they are spending up to six months in the US without working. Most people can't afford to spend six months at home without working, let alone in a foreign country. Because many B-1 holders were merely too lazy to get a proper working visa, INS tends to be suspicious.

What constitutes work becomes an important question at a port of entry. Simply put, work means that your activity takes an American job. While it's clear that meetings, sales calls and scientific collaborations don't constitute work, the closer one gets to handling machinery, products or directing subordinate employees the harder it is to convince the INS inspector that you aren't working in the US.

Legally, B-1 visitors may handle equipment or products for demonstration purposes. This leaves the B-1 visitor with the problem of convincing the INS inspector that he only incidentally handles the product. Common sense dictates that the more time you spend in the US and the closer your activities come to handling products or machinery, the higher your burden of proof at a port of entry.

APPLICATION PROCEDURES AND STRATEGY

All nationalities except Canadians must apply for a B-1 visa at a US consulate. Provide the consular officer with background data to support the B-1 visa application. Important documentation includes:

- A detailed itinerary.

- Reasons for needing more than 90 days, if you are eligible for visa waiver, to conduct your business in the US.

- Proof that you will be paid from abroad.

- Proof that you are either an independent business person or that a foreign employer controls your activities.

Even if the consul issues the B-1 visa, you must still convince the INS inspector upon arrival in the US that you qualify for the B-1 visa at the time of entry. As in all visa matters, it's a two-step process: first you must make your case to the consul, after which you make your case to the INS inspector. You must pass both tests in order to enter the US.

Canadians merely state the purpose of their business trip at a port of entry. If the reasons are satisfactory, the inspector admits the Canadian without a B-1 visa or I-94 or other documentation. The maximum stay period is six months.

Assessing B-1 advantages
Because of uncertain results at US ports of entry I only recommend B-1 visas in special cases. Scientific collaborations, sales calls, work on a specific collaborative effort between a foreign and US company make good B-1 scenarios.

When in doubt try to obtain longer-term nonimmigrant working visas. B-1 visas often involve borderline situations where no clear definition of work exists. Most of us think we work when on a business trip. But you can't work while on a B-1 visa. It's easy to get confused and even easier for INS to show you the door based on your confusion. Remember, INS can remove anybody they suspect of misrepresenting the purpose of their trip to the US without a hearing.

Although B-1 visa holders may avoid US income tax liability, it may be worth applying for a long-term working visa and paying the tax, to ensure that you can go about your business in the US without fear of immigration problems. The time, expense and disruption to your business resulting from being delayed or refused entry to the US may exceed the costs associated with a nonimmigrant working visa.

4

Travelling for Pleasure: The B–2 Visa

Since the advent of the visa waiver program, fewer people need **B-2 Visitor for Pleasure** visas. (Visa waivers are available for people from Canada, most European countries, and Japan.) After all, how many people take vacations that last more than two weeks, let alone more than the 90 days permitted under visa waiver? If you are eligible for a visa waiver, consuls usually will not issue a B-2 visa.

Normally, families or couples from non-visa waiver countries coming to the US for short vacations or even for a summer tour face few problems entering on visa waiver or obtaining B-2 visas. The B-2 application procedures are the same as for B-1 visas.

IDENTIFYING PROBLEM AREAS

Single young men and women and student-aged children face intense scrutiny when applying for a B-2 visa, or when applying for permission to enter the US. Student-aged children come to the US with or without parents, often posing as tourists, with the intention of enrolling in school. Mothers often stay in the US illegally to take care of the child. No visa category permits mothers to care for children going to American schools.

STUDENTS

If a child enters the US as a tourist without an endorsed visa, and later attempts to change to student status, the

INS may find that the child misrepresented his intentions for entering the US and deny the change of B-2 to F-1 student status request. Even if the INS approves the change of status from B-2 to F-1 student, and subsequently the student applies for a visa, most consuls will resist issuing an F-1 student visa for the same reasons. This will mean that the student cannot leave the US to apply for a visa with any assurance of being able to return. Students often find themselves 'locked' within the US, separated from their families, while holding an illegal visa that will expire well before the school term is completed.

Student-aged children intending to enrol in an American school should tell the consul the truth. If convinced of a child's student bonafides and financial support, the consul will issue a B-2 visa endorsed 'prospective student', or the like. Such an endorsement permits the children and parents to find a suitable school for the student. If all goes well the child may change to F-1 status while in the US, and later return home to apply for an F-1 student visa. Effective documentation for prospective F-1 students using a B-2 visa to shop for schools includes:

- academic references

- a list of prospective schools

- letters of invitation to visit schools

- proof of arrangements for care and support while attending school in the US.

YOUNG ADULTS

Young single men and women face a different problem. Many singles come to the US for no other purpose than to marry their way to a green card. The high incidence of singles coming to the US for this reason has influenced

INS enforcement policy. Unfortunately, this policy creates difficulties for young singles who have legitimate reasons for visiting the US.

Yet there are ways for young singles to come to the US for legitimate travel reasons. It's important that they carefully document plans to return home following a vacation. Effective documentation includes:

• proof of a job or business at home

• proof of family ties at home (list family members)

• proof that you are pursuing an education at home

• a detailed itinerary of the US trip

• letters of invitation or reference from US citizens or permanent residents

• proof that you can support yourself while in the US.

In other words, provide proof that you have too much to lose by leaving home for an extended period.

5

Entering the US as a Fiancé(e)

Marriage to a US citizen qualifies you for a green card. If the marriage occurs abroad the green card petition must be filed through a US Consulate with jurisdiction over the applicant's place of residence. The procedures usually take between six to nine months to complete. Many newlyweds, for a variety of reasons, don't relish the idea of six months of separation or six months or so of waiting before they can enter the US as a married couple.

Although the same process that takes six to eight months abroad takes 12–18 months in the US, the applicant may work and live in the US from the date of filing. Thus the lengthy processing period is not as inconvenient as it would seem. Those who apply abroad must wait outside the US during the entire processing period. As a result, many newlyweds prefer to undertake the entire green card application process in the US, so that they can live together and work while they patiently wait for the bureaucracy to grind out the green card approval notice.

The INS will not admit people who intend to live in the US permanently as a nonimmigrant. The choice is:

- to file the green card application abroad and come to the US as a permanent resident

- bring your fiancé(e) or spouse to the US using a K-1 visa

- or to come to the US as a non-immigrant tourist or worker, then marry and finally file for the green card in the US.

In the latter case, if the INS knew all the facts they

would deny entry and possibly bar entry for five years under summary removal procedures. One may not enter the US as a nonimmigrant with the intent to live in the US permanently.

THE FIANCÉ(E) VISA CATEGORY

Rather than force people to lie about the purpose of their entry to the US, in 1970 Congress created the K-1 or fiancé(e) visa category. The K-1 visa avoids the risk of being denied entry to the US or worse. The K-1 visa permits a fiancé(e) to enter the US as long as the marriage takes place within 90 days of entry. The visa may not be extended so be sure to marry within 90 days. The applicant may work in the US during the 90-day period. Immediately after the marriage, the couple may file the green card petition, Form I-130, and the adjustment of status petition I-485 with INS. The K-1 visa tends to reduce the INS processing period because the K-1 visa application process requires much of the same information that the INS requires for the green card petition.

The K-1 visa was recently extended to married persons. A person married to a US citizen may now qualify for K-1 status to legally enter the US to adjust to permanent residence status rather than waiting abroad for the completion of the Embassy procedures. Married people may now adjust to permanent residence status abroad or in the US.

FOLLOWING PROCEDURES

The US citizen side of the equation files Form I-129F on behalf of the intended or spouse by mail at one of the four INS regional processing centres. This form requires personal data for each applicant, proof that the applicants have met within the two years prior to application and a statement that the applicants intend to marry within 90 days of entry to the US. INS will make exceptions for arranged marriages if the applicants can show that arranged marriages are a family custom.

If the petition is approved, INS will send the file to the Consulate nearest the residence of the alien fiancé(e) or spouse. The Consul will conduct security clearance procedures and then schedule an interview, much like a permanent residence interview. The applicant must supply pictures, a medical exam, and an affidavit of support. The green card interview and K-1 interview procedures are almost identical.

If the Consul issues the visa, the supporting documents are put in a sealed envelope for presentation to the INS at the port of entry. This same package can be used for the adjustment of status and green card application with INS after the marriage.

The fiancé(e) has four months from the date of visa petition approval to apply for the K-1 visa at a US Consulate. Although the four-month period may be extended, each extension request casts doubt on the ultimate intention to marry in the US.

The fiancé(e) must either marry within the 90-day period or leave the US. If the fiancé(e) leaves prior to the expiration of the 90-day period and returns, he or she will only be admitted for the balance of the first 90-day period.

Fiancé(e) dependants receive a K-2 visa, which does not permit employment but does permit attending school.

SUMMARY

- The K-1 visa is the legal way to enter the US with the intention of marrying a US citizen.

- Those who don't want to marry within 90 days need to use a B1/2 or nonimmigrant work visa and to hope that the INS inspectors don't ask the right question.

6

Temporary Working Visas

International organisations and corporations use nonimmigrant working visas to staff US operations. Investors use nonimmigrant visas for themselves and employees sent to the US to monitor investments. US employers use nonimmigrant visas to fill skill shortages in their companies. Many people use nonimmigrant working visas as a stepping stone to permanent residence status and then citizenship. People commonly obtain a nonimmigrant work visa so that they can remain in the US while applying or waiting for a green card.

This chapter defines the basic terms and concepts concerning the most commonly used nonimmigrant work visas: **E**, **H** and **L**. Subsequent chapters describe less frequently used categories along with the strategy and approach for specific situations.

GETTING THE GENERAL OUTLINE

The US maintains two interdependent nonimmigrant working visa systems. E visas are the product of treaties, negotiated between the US and other countries and administered by the Department of State through embassies and consulates. Congress created the other commonly used nonimmigrant work visas – H and L – through domestic law. The INS serves as the lead agency for administering H and L visas or other visas created by domestic law. Read this chapter before you read the chapters discussing how to staff companies, make investments in the US, or obtain a green card.

Most companies use a combination of E-1/2, H-1B, L-1A and L-1B visas to staff their US operations. The same person may qualify for an E visa category, or an H or L visa category. The combination of the H and L categories describes the same work activities as the E categories. E visas include professionals, managers, executives and essential skill employees, whereas H and L include professionals, executives, managers and specialised knowledge employees. Differences in corporate ownership and organisation, convenience, or the enforcement policies of the initial governmental agency you'll be working with, the INS or Department of State, determine whether to apply for an E visa or an H or L visa.

UNDERSTANDING THE TERMINOLOGY

Professionals

The term 'professional' refers to four-year university graduates who work in professional positions. These include lawyers, accountants, engineers, market researchers and economists. Depending on individual circumstances, a professional may quality for H-1B status, E status or even L-1A manager status.

Executive/manager

The term 'executive' is used literally. The term 'manager' refers to someone who directs or monitors the activities of other professionals, managers and supervisors. Managers are not involved in the direct manufacture of a product or provision of a service. Most executives and managers use E or L-1A manager visas.

International organisation

The term 'international organisation' refers to US companies having 50 per cent or more common ownership with a foreign company or individuals. Ownership may be traced through unlimited tiers of companies or individuals as long as one can ultimately establish 50 per cent or more common ownership.

Essential skill and specialised knowledge

'Essential skill' (E visa) or 'specialised knowledge' (L-1B visa) applicants possess knowledge critical to the success of the US (E visa) or beneficial to US competitiveness (L-1B visa). When essential skills or specialized knowledge applicants also serve in executive/managerial or professional positions, they may also qualify for H-1B, L-1A or E visa status as professionals or executive managers.

L VISAS: INTRA-COMPANY TRANSFER

The L visa category includes executive, manager or specialized knowledge applicants who transfer within an international organisation. To qualify for any L category the visa applicant must transfer within the same international organisation. The applicant must work in a qualifying capacity (as an executive, manager or specialized knowledge employee) for a foreign member of the international organization, for one of three years preceding the transfer to the American member of the international organisation in the same capacity. L visa applicants file Form I-129 and the L supplement with the INS.

As an example, a manager joined the foreign parent company in 1991 and resigned in June 1993. In June 1994 the foreign parent company rehired the manager to transfer to the US, then filed its L-1A petition. The manager meets the one-year test because he worked as a manager in the foreign parent company one of the three years prior to the petition filing date. If the applicant fails the one-year requirement, consider E or H-1B visa status.

To qualify as an international organisation the parent company must establish a branch office, subsidiary company or affiliate company in the US. From an immigration point of view, it makes little difference whether a branch, subsidiary or affiliated company is formed as long as the arrangement qualifies as an international organisation for L-1 purposes. International organisations are as follows.

Branch office in the US

A branch office refers to the parent company registering itself to do business in the US, as opposed to forming a subsidiary or affiliate.

Subsidiary company

A subsidiary for L visa purposes is a US company owned 50 per cent or more by a foreign corporation.

Affiliated company

An affiliated company is a business linked by at least 50 per cent common ownership to the foreign parent. For L-1 purposes the foreign parent must directly or indirectly control the US branch, subsidiary or affiliate. Control in this case generally means 50 per cent or more direct or indirect ownership.

A 50-50 joint venture between a foreign and American company may be an affiliate of the foreign company since the foreign company owns half of the US business. The joint venture could be a partnership between the US company and the foreign company's wholly-owned US subsidiary. Or it could be a corporation owned half by US shareholders or companies, and half by the foreign company or its subsidiary. Many foreign companies transfer managers, executives or specialized knowledge persons to US joint-venture operations.

TREATY TRADER/INVESTOR BASIC TERMINOLOGY

The following discussion involves the workings of the treaty trader/investor treaties. It's difficult to understand how to use E visa without some background on the subject.

The E categories include executives, managers, professional and essential skill applicants hired by a company controlled by at least 50 per cent of the treaty nationals involved in qualifying trade or investment. The E visa applicant must be of the same nationality as the controlling ownership. The American E visa employer qualifies as a treaty company on the basis of the nationality of its shareholders as well as the qualifying trade or investment.

E visa processing

E visa processing consists of two basic steps. First, the US company must be qualified as a **Treaty Trader** or **Treaty Investor**. The US company must prove it made a substantial investment or controls substantial qualifying trade. Secondly, the company must prove the applicant qualifies as an executive, manager or essential skill employee.

The applicant, if in the US, may change to E status by filing for an INS change of status on Form I-129, Application for Nonimmigrant Workers, with the E supplement. If the applicant works abroad the application must be filed with a consul. Forms, procedures and enforcement policies vary among the consular offices.

The treaty national employees of a treaty trader company receive E-1 visas. The treaty national employees of a treaty investor company obtain E-2 visas. When the same company qualifies for both E-1 and E-2 status, the consul will only accord the applicant one status. For example, the United Kingdom is a 'treaty country', thus making a UK-controlled company in the US a 'treaty company' and a UK citizen working for the treaty company a 'treaty national'.

Note that green card holders count as US workers for E visa purposes regardless of their nationality. In the above example, a UK green card holder may not qualify as a treaty national as he or she is considered a 'US person'.

The treaties

The 'treaty' refers to a **Friendship Commerce and Navigation Treaty (FCN)** or a **Bilateral Investment Treaty (BIT)** between the US and a foreign country. Such treaties contain agreements concerning trade, investing, shipping, aviation and staffing of operations in each country. The

US has negotiated such treaties with over 50 countries, including Japan, Taiwan, Korea, Thailand, most European countries and Canada.

The US originally negotiated FCN and BIT treaties to assure equal access to foreign markets and prevent arbitrary limitations on the number of treaty nationals permitted to staff foreign operations. Now that the US runs a trade deficit, FCN and BIT treaties tend to protect foreign nationals doing business in the US. Twenty-five years ago, the reverse was true.

Many countries created arbitrary ratios (such as one American technician per five Japanese technicians) to assure local control of foreign enterprises. FCN and BIT treaties prevented this practice by giving treaty traders or investors the opportunity to staff foreign operations with qualified persons of their 'choice'.

Although there is no legal limit on the number of E visa employees, over the years the State Department limited the treaty company's 'choice' by imposing training requirements, suggesting that treaty companies hire more US workers, or by strictly defining the classes of eligible workers. Today, 'choice' means that the treaty company may employ as many applicants as it wants as long as the consul agrees.

CONTROL AND OWNERSHIP OF A US TREATY COMPANY

'Control' refers to 50 per cent or more treaty national ownership of a US company. Japan is a treaty country, and a joint venture based in the US and controlled by 50 per cent or more of Japanese treaty nationals qualifies as a treaty company. US subsidiaries of companies such as Sony and Honda are treaty companies. Public companies generally take the nationality of their primary place of incorporation or the location of the stock exchange that trades most of their shares.

Subsequent changes in corporate ownership by either the parent or US treaty company may affect treaty status.

Treaty nationals must at all times control the US treaty company. If at any time treaty national ownership dips below 50 per cent, the US treaty company loses its treaty status. Fifty-fifty joint ventures risk losing treaty status if US shareholders purchase additional shares from the treaty national shareholders, thus changing the ownership ratio.

TREATY TRADER: E-1 VISA

Service and trading companies may qualify for E-1 treaty trader status. 'Trade' signifies trade in goods and trade in services. Banks, financial service companies, software firms, attorneys, accountants and the like, along with companies trading goods, may qualify for E-1 treaty trader status.

'**Treaty trade**' means substantial trade primarily between the treaty national countries. 'Primarily' means that 50 per cent or more of the treaty company trade (the US operation) is between the treaty company and the treaty country. If Honda USA wants to be a treaty trader company, over half of its imports and exports must be between the US and Japan.

Treaty trade must be substantial, though there is no specific monetary amount to define 'substantial'. Enforcement varies among US consuls world-wide as local economic conditions dictate the definition of substantial treaty trade.

In Japan, Taiwan, Korea and Europe, substantial trade generally involves many small annual transactions of at least $500,000, or a few large annual transactions in the millions of dollars. In lesser developed countries, consuls often approve E-1 visas for smaller amounts of trade. Generally, the poorer the country the lower the trade threshold. Consuls focus on business activity and try to limit treaty trader status to active and on-going business ventures, not short-term projects.

Direct trade
Only direct trade qualifies for E-1 purposes. For example, US-incorporated Japanese treaty Company A sells to US-

incorporated UK treaty Company B. Company B exports to the UK. Company A cannot claim B's exports for E-1 trade purposes even if the British buyer is A's parent company. If Company A wants E-1 status, it must make sure the exports are shipped under its name.

Trade primarily between the US and a treaty country
Trade between the US and a treaty country must exceed 50 per cent of the US treaty company's total world-wide trade. 'Trade' is defined by the US treaty company's commerce with a treaty country. In one case, a Taiwanese company exports from the US to Taiwan through a branch office in America. As the US dollar lost value, trade between the US and Taiwan fell to less than 50 per cent of the company's total trade. Because of this drop in trade the company lost its E-1 visa status.

Doing business in the US through a US-incorporated subsidiary prevents the above scenario. A branch office is part of the parent company, not a separate company. Thus the parent is also the treaty company. A branch office must compare its trade with the treaty country to the parent company's total world-wide trade. A US subsidiary is a separate company, not part of the parent company. In the case of a subsidiary company, 'treaty trade' refers to the subsidiary company's trade with the treaty country. As long as the US subsidiary does 50 per cent or more of its import/export business with the treaty country (not necessarily the parent company), the trade will be primarily between the US and the treaty country.

TREATY INVESTOR E-2

E-2 status requires a substantial treaty investment. A 'substantial investment' in a business generally involves at least $200,000. Payment may be in cash or a combination of cash and debt. Depending on national conditions and individual circumstances, the US Consulate may approve cases for smaller ventures. Although there is no statutory minimum investment, the smaller the investment the tougher it is to get visa approval. Funds must come from the treaty country of the investor, and borrowed funds may not be secured by assets of the treaty investment.

The smaller the cost of the business the higher the percentage of cash investment required. Consular officers usually require a cash investment of 65 per cent, or $130,000, for a business that costs $200,000. A million-dollar investment requires a smaller investment percentage. Again, these are only general guidelines. Consuls base their decisions on the specific facts of each case.

BASIC REQUIREMENTS OF H-1B VISAS: FOR PROFESSIONAL WORKERS

The applicant must have professional qualifications and work in a job requiring these qualifications. For example, a staff economist should have a Bachelor of Arts degree in Economics. The term 'specialty worker' used in the regulations really means 'professional worker'. If the applicant does not have a university degree, it's best to find an alternative visa status. The regulations exempt people with ten or more years of work experience from the degree requirement. However, if there's another visa choice, use it. Qualifying for H-1B status without a university degree is very difficult.

The US government limits the number of H-1B visas to 195,000 per year until 30 September 2003. Until 1998 the quota was 55,000. The increase in usage comes primarily from the high-tech industries. Because the size of the quota is a hotly debated polical issue, one can not predict the size of future quotas.

As long as computer and biotech continue to grow the quota will probably continue to be insufficient. Those who can plan ahead should file as close as possible to the beginning of the government fiscal year, 1 October.

In order to win passage of the legislation to increase the quota, organised labour demanded an additional filing fee of $1,000 to pay for worker training and scholarships. This additional $1,000 fee is due for all initial H-1B petitions and the first extension. All companies except educational institutions and non-profit companies must pay the additional filing fee.

H-1B employers

H-1B employers may be completely US owned, completely foreign owned, or a combination of the two. An H-1B employer must be incorporated or otherwise licensed to do business in the US, *ie* an American employer. An American employer, or a US agent of a foreign employer, must petition for H-1B and L status. Foreign employers may petition for E status. The term 'US employer' refers to the place of incorporation or licensure, not ownership. A totally foreign owned US corporation is a US employer because it is incorporated in the US.

The Labour Conditions Application process

H-1B employers must file a Labour Conditions Application (LCA) form with the US Department of Labor, post the form on the company bulletin board for ten days, or give the form to a union representative prior to filing for H-1B. The LCA form requires the employer to disclose the H-1B applicant's job title and salary to ensure there is no labour problem, and to promise to pay the H-1B applicant the prevailing wage. The LCA procedures add approximately 30 days to H-1B visa processing. Only after LCA approval may employers petition the INS for H-1B status. Allow 90 days for H-1B processing, in addition to the LCA processing.

'Prevailing wage' is the salary that the Department of Labor determines most people in the work area earn for a particular job. Employers must document how they determined the prevailing wage. It's best to obtain a prevailing wage determination from the State Department of Labor before filing an H-1B petition. American companies looking for low-priced foreign labour often have trouble with the prevailing wage rate.

Many companies resist telling US workers the salary of

a new foreign worker. However, the Department of Labor may levy fines and/or prohibit the employer from applying for H-1B visas for not posting the LCA notice where all employees can see it, failing to disclose accurate information, or not paying the prevailing wage.

'Dependent employers', or companies of 50 or more employees with 15 per cent or more foreign workers, in addition to meeting the prevailing wage standards must attest that they recruited for the position prior to hiring the H-1B worker and offered the position to equally or more qualified US workers, and that the employer has not laid off a US worker in the same position as the intended H-1B within 90 days before and after filing the H-1B petition.

There is a sliding scale for smaller companies. 'Dependent employers' also include companies with one to 25 total employees with nine or more H-1B employees and companies with 12–25 total employees with 14 or more H-1B employees. INS waives the 'dependent employers' attestation when the H-1B applicant has a Masters Degree or better or earns $60,000 or more per annum. The 'dependent employers' attestation, although difficult to enforce, gives the Department of Labor an additional level to discourage the use of foreign labour.

The H-1B attestation requirements are unavoidable, the only alternative being to use another visa category. However, you don't always have that choice.

PROFESSIONAL LICENCES

H-1B professionals must either be licensed in the state of intended employment or be exempt from the licence requirement. State law defines the professions which require a licence. In most cases, professionals such as engineers, lawyers, accountants or architects, who work for a company and do not serve the public, don't require state licences. One must consult state law to determine licence requirements.

As an example, companies often transfer a person to

oversee the legal matters of their US operations. In many countries, universities offer an undergraduate programme in commercial law. Commonly, graduates never take a bar exam or obtain a licence to practise law. In-house lawyers or businessmen with law degrees qualify for H-1B status.

The typical applicant usually holds a commercial law degree and has worked with the company's benefit programmes, labour relations, regulatory compliance, or contractual negotiations. The applicant never took a licence to practise law. The applicant will be transferred to the US subsidiary to coordinate subsidiary and home-office legal affairs, monitor regulatory compliance, engage outside professionals on an as-needed basis, coordinate home-office and subsidiary benefit plans, and monitor compliance with US civil rights anti-discrimination rules. This applicant doesn't need a licence to practise law because he serves his company, not the public.

H-1B Portability Rules

Generally H-1B visas are only valid for work for the petitioning employer and are only valid for six years. There are two exceptions to the general rule. An H-1B employee may change jobs and work for the new employer using the old H-1B visa once the new H-1B petition has been filed. The applicant may work for the new employer from the time of filing the new petition without waiting for INS approval. Initial H-1B applicants must wait for visa approval to commence employment.

Employees who have applied for permanent residence status may extend their H-1B visas in one-year increments beyond the six-year limit if their labour certification has been approved and the I-140 preference petition has been filed and a year has lapsed from the date the labour certification was originally filed.

Pointers for individuals using H-1B professional status to work in the US

- You must arrange a job with a definite offer of employment before applying for the H-1B visa.

- Although you may apply from abroad, you need the job offer first.

- Lawyers generally can't help you find a job. Find a job first, then call the lawyer to help with the visa process.

- Negotiate an employment contract. H-1B employers must pay your airfare home if you get fired.

- H-1B visas only last six years. Make sure you have enough time (allow two years to be safe) to obtain a green card before the H-1B validity period terminates, otherwise you must rely on the portability rules which are difficult to manage.

- Professional and scientific university degrees make for an easier case than liberal arts degrees.

- Young, inexperienced applicants must convince the consular officer that the job is *bona fide*, not an accommodation to the applicant.

- Prepare evidence that the employer recruited for the position. This may include letters of recommendation, or a detailed job description on the employer's stationery with the reasons the employer wants your services.

- H-1B visas are subject to an annual quota of 195,000. This quota is often oversubscribed by the middle of the government fiscal year. It is best to apply as close as possible to 1 October, the first day of the government fiscal year.

Pointers for employers using H-1B visas for professional workers

- You must pay the prevailing wage. The trend is towards higher prevailing wages, hence there is a temptation to cheat. Don't do it!

- If the state job service prevailing wage is too high, you may rely on private employment surveys. Although the Department of Labor must accept private surveys, the best proof that you paid the prevailing wage is a certification from the state job service. Private surveys save time and you eliminate dealing with the state job service, but they don't afford the best protection against complaints from US workers that you paid a foreigner less than the prevailing wage. On the other hand, it's often your only choice, because state job services frequently believe the prevailing wages are higher than the wage you would be willing to pay.

- Young H-1B employees with little working experience often ultimately want a green card. Because they can't count experience gained with the petitioning employer (see Chapter 9 on labour certification), they must find a different employer for the green card process. You may invest in an employee only to lose him later. Investigate an employee's desire for a green card and the likelihood for success before you make the hire.

- Your prospective H-1B employee may be in the US on a tourist or student visa. Don't hire the H-1B employee until the H-1B visa is approved, unless the employee has a different visa permitting him to work for your company. Allow 120 days for H-1B visa processing.

- H-1 dependent employers should save all resumés and advertisements to prove they recruited for the position before hiring the H-1B employee.

- Remember the $1,000 additional filing fee.

- Although part-time employment is permitted, employers must state their intention to hire the employee part-time on the application form.

KNOWING WHEN TO USE H, L OR E

Corporate organisation, convenience, or the applicant's background may dictate whether to apply for E, H or L categories. Each of the E, H and L categories permits the applicant to work in the US and allows spouses and children to live or study (but not work) in the US. Dependent children must be under age 21. Children over 21 need an independent visa status. All three categories are employer-specific. The holder of the visa may only work for the sponsoring employer.

Assuming you may choose between E, H or L status, consider the following guidelines:

- E visas may be extended as long as the US business remains viable. There is no limit to extensions of the visa. Most consuls issue E visas for five-year periods.

- L visas are limited to seven years for executives and managers and five years for specialized knowledge. H visas are limited to six years for professionals. Most initial L-1 and H-1B visas are valid for three years.

- If you ultimately want a green card, try to arrange your affairs so that you are transferred in a managerial or executive capacity within an international organisation.

- If none of the above matters to you, apply for the category that affords the fastest and easiest processing. This depends on a comparison of the enforcement policies and service standards of the consulate nearest your home to those of the INS service centre controlling the area of your intended employment.

SUMMARISING ELIGIBILITY FOR E, H AND L VISA HOLDERS

L visas accommodate transfers within an international organisation, and E visas accommodate citizens or companies of the treaty country involved in qualifying trade or investment. H-1B professionals may work for any incorporated or licensed US company that requires the services of a professional. The definitions overlap and the same person may qualify for one or more visa categories.

The following scenarios clarify company requirements for the E, H and L visas. If the US employer is:

- A member of an L visa international organisation and qualifies for either E-1 or E-2 status, the company may use L, H and E visas.

- Not a member of an L visa international organisation but qualifies for either E-1 or E-2 status, the company may use E or H visas.

- Not a member of an L visa international organisation, and does not qualify for E-1 or E-2 status, the company may only use H visas.

In rare cases, consider O, P and Q visas. See Chapter 11.

Pay to Play
Due to complaints about slow processing times, INS initated expedited processing fees. Once can pay an additional $1,000 along with Form 907 to obtain 15-day processing service. INS promises an answer, not necessarily a decision within 15 days of receipt of the petition. An 'answer' may merely be a request for more information. Expedited processing is now available for most H, L and E category visa petitions.

7

Sending Staff to a New Business in America

Typically clients come to my office and say, 'I want to open my business in America. How do I do it?' At this point there is usually no more than an idea or business plan to work with.

ESTABLISHING THE US COMPANY FIRST

No matter what visa alternative you ultimately choose you will need to establish a US company licensed to do business in a particular state. The INS will not consider most business oriented visa petitions unless a US company exists. Although there are reasons to establish partnerships, joint ventures or even to use individual ownership, in most cases it's best to form a limited company or a corporation.

The INS is familiar with corporations. It is not familiar with limited partnerships, complicated general partnerships, and limited liability companies. If you can help it, don't complicate your petition.

Simply put, shareholders of corporations only risk their capital in the company. Partners or sole proprietors place all their assets at risk in the event of a law suit or business failure. Limited liability companies, Sub S corporations and limited partnerships are hybrids between corporate and individual ownership.

Considering death taxes

Although a discussion of the tax advantages and disadvantages of the various forms of ownership is beyond the scope of this book, a short explanation of death taxes is in order. The US levies estate or death tax upon the death of a US tax resident. US tax residents include some nonimmigrants, permanent residents and citizens. The estate tax on nonimmigrants and permanent residents is much higher than the estate tax on citizens.

Corporations have eternal life. Individual shareholders will die but not the corporation. A corporation owned by a foreign corporation doesn't even have a shareholder that can die. If there's no death there's no estate tax. Using a foreign corporation to own the shares of the US corporation not only works best for most immigration purposes, but also offers the possibility of reducing estate taxes.

FORMING THE CORPORATION

Incorporating a company in the US is a simple matter; there is no federal or national registration. Incorporate at the state level, not with the federal government in Washington D.C. Most states use similar rules and procedures. No states conduct background checks, limit entry into particular businesses or require a minimum amount of capital.

Most European and Asian countries require maintenance of a minimum amount of capital in return for granting the shareholders the rights of limited liability. The US grants corporate shareholders limited liability free of charge.

Foreigners may serve as officers or directors without restriction. Officers and directors do not have to reside in the state of incorporation or in the US.

Additionally, apply for a tax identification number as well as state and local business licences. Accountants normally take care of the initial registrations. Normally, processing takes a matter of a few weeks. Corporate filing fees vary from state to state; most states charge under $1,000. You can incorporate without the services of an attorney, but it's usually not worth the time and risk of undertaking an unfamiliar task to save $1,000 or so in attorney fees.

FINDING PREMISES FOR DOING BUSINESS

There's no choice; INS will also not consider business oriented petitions without proof of a place to do business. Don't use an apartment or residence.

APPLYING FOR THE WORKING VISA

Once the office and the company is established you may apply for your working visa. Most people apply for either L-1A international manager, E1/2 treaty trader or investor, or H-1B speciality occupations.

Most companies apply for L-1A visas because this category was designed to accommodate start-up companies. The L-1A permits a manager to come to the US for an initial one-year period to establish the enterprise. E1/12 visas require existing trade or investment irrevocably committed to the enterprise. The H-1B was not designed for start-ups but can be used at a pinch. The L-1A requires a company licence, secured premises, a reasonable business plan and proof of the ability to execute the business plan.

The foreign parent company must prove that it has sufficient capital and experience to support the fledgling US business. The visa applicant must be a managerial or executive employee who worked for the corporate group for one of the three years prior to the petition date.

CASE STUDY

A foreign chemical company plans to enter the US market. It already sells products through a US distributor, and wants to establish a US subsidiary to ultimately purchase the distributor, and establish sales and manufacturing operations in the US.

The transfer candidate, a 35-year-old manager with ten years' experience with the parent company, will be the only employee during the start-up period. The candidate manages export sales to the US for the parent company, and has worked with the US distributor. While working in the US the candidate will conduct market research and prepare for the takeover of the distributor. The foreign company leases office space from the distributor and has established a US subsidiary corporation.

This should be a textbook case of proper eligibility for the L-1A visa category. There are a US company, a parent company with money and experience, a leased office and a verifiable business plan. Even though the foreign company was a multi-billion dollar company, the INS questioned the petitioner's ability to carry out the business plan. We pointed out that the parent company, a multi-national corporation, had more than sufficient cash, savings and experience to open a new branch office and the petition was approved.

Learning some lessons
There are two lessons to be learned. The people adjudicating petitions for INS are often inexperienced, poorly trained and never have enough time to thoroughly read the file. Hence INS often asks for information they already have, and many of the INS requests for further information are generated from a word processor and have nothing to do with the instant file. Rather than getting upset, it's best to give INS what they want, even if that means sending the same document again and pointing out that it was already in the file.

The other lesson to be learned is that the INS scrutinises applications involving start-up companies because start-ups often don't make it and are often established for the primary purpose of obtaining a green card, rather than for a business purpose. There's an easy solution to this problem: send money. Send enough money to the new US company to cover operations for a year. Also supply a detailed budget of the first two or three years' operations, showing where the money comes from. Although the L-1A category does not require a specific amount of initial capital, applicants must prove the ability to sustain the company during the first year of operations. Put another way, you need to pay to play.

EXPLORING ALTERNATIVES TO THE L-1A APPROACH

Using the E1/2 visa

The parent company could have capitalised the US subsidiary and signed a purchase and sale agreement to purchase the US distributor. Depending on the amount, the capital transfer, coupled with the purchase and sale agreement and the existing trade between the parent company and the US, should permit one E1 or E2 manager, assuming the appropriate treaty nationality, to come to the US to establish the subsidiary company.

The E1/2 visa alternative must be considered when the managerial transferee does not have one year's managerial experience abroad as required for the L-1A visa. Because the E1/2 visa categories were designed to accommodate existing trade or investment, the petition must demonstrate a higher showing of commitment of capital or existence of trade than in the case of the L-1A visa.

Using the example above, the L-1A visa application does not require a commitment to purchase the US distributor. The E visa petition either requires proof of existing trade or proof of a contract, backed with at least a deposit, to purchase the US distributor.

The H-1B visa offers an interesting alternative to the L-1A visa for start-up companies. Employees with a professional level of education, Baccalaureate degree or better, who come to work in a professional position for US employers, qualify for H-1B status.

Using the H-1B visa

An overview of the H-1B regulations suggests that the US employer is an existing and active business with other US employees. On the other hand the regulations merely state that the employer must be a US employer. A US employer is any company formed and licensed to do business in the US, regardless of ownership. Thus the start-up company described in the above example qualifies as a US employer. Until INS changes the rules, H-1B visas are viable in start-up company situations.

The first person to staff the start-up usually conducts market research and formulates the plan for launching the business. Depending upon the scope of the project, market research often requires professional expertise. Bachelor of Arts degrees in marketing, business, commercial law, economics, political science, accounting and finance logically support business planning or market research positions. In technical areas, market research may require an engineering or other scientific degree.

The H-1B visa provides two advantages over L-1A in the start-up situation. The INS usually issues the initial H-1B visa for three years, not an initial one-year period as in the L-1A, and there is no requirement to hire employees as in the case of the L-1A. On the down side, the H-1B filing fee is $1,000 higher than the L-1A filing fee and a corporate officer will have to sign the H-1B labour conditions attestation forms.

MAKING THE FINAL CHOICE

The L-1A is the preferred method for new companies because the regulations specifically accommodate start-up companies. Furthermore, it is easier to obtain a green card starting from L-1A status. The H-1B is a last resort to be considered after L-1A and E1/2 visa alternatives.

EXTENDING YOUR US STAY AFTER THE ONE-YEAR PERIOD

Start-up company L-1A visas have an initial validity period of one year, not three years as in other L-1A situations. The L-1A manager must conduct active business and hire employees within the one-year period. Remember, L-1A managers must oversee other managers, supervisors or professionals. At a minimum, the manager must make tangible progress towards establishing the business. At the end of the first year the L-1A visa can be extended for up to two three-year periods.

H-1B visa holders are limited to six consecutive years in the US. The L-1A visa holders are restricted to seven consecutive years in the US. At the end of the maximum validity period they may change to any other status than H-1B or L-1A, often E1/2, or they must leave the US for at least one year before reapplying in H-1B or L-1A status.

L-1A visa renewals become difficult unless the manager makes tangible progress in establishing an active US business. Tangible progress includes:

- hiring two or three people

- showing a trend of increasing gross sales

- acquisition of necessary capital assets

- or construction/remodel of premises or a factory.

Larger companies fare better in this regard as they can say their lack of progress is due to bigger projects which take more time to launch. And they can easily prove they have the capital necessary to continue the project. Small companies must often reapply as a start-up or change to H-1B status. E1/2 visa will not work without active trade or a substantial investment, in which case there should be no problem extending the L-1A visa.

Understanding the one-year rule

INS designed the one-year 'doing business' requirement to force the applicant company to show good faith in efforts to establish itself in the US. In the 1980s many Taiwanese companies established US subsidiary 'shell' companies as a vehicle to move children to the US to study and to later apply for a green card. The INS established the one-year doing business rule for start-up companies to curtail this abuse.

Russian and PRC Chinese companies tend to follow the trail blazed by their Taiwanese predecessors. The INS tends to not only question Russian and PRC Chinese start-up company applications, but often sends the files to field investigators who visit the premises in the home country and the US to check the bonafides of the visa petition. This practice not only delays processing but also creates some unfortunate results. We have had to appeal several cases where INS checked the wrong address or the manager was simply out of the office when the INS investigator knocked on the door.

Technically, INS must consider mitigating circumstances when determining compliance with the one-year of doing business rule. Reasonable excuses include bad luck, unforeseen delays, and the fact that some businesses take longer to establish than others. The INS tends to take a harsh and simplistic view. If after one year there are no new employees and no trend of increasing gross sales, no visa extension will be issued.

PASSING THE ONE YEAR OF BUSINESS HURDLE

With an extended L-1A visa safely in hand the employer must decide what to do at the end of the seven-year maximum L-1A validity period. There are three reasonable choices:

1. Rotate L-1A managers. Continue using L-1A visas for successor managers.

2. If eligible change to E1/2 visa at the end of the

maximum validity period. The E1/2 has no maximum validity period.

3. Apply for a green card after one year of doing business in the US. See Chapter 8.

WHAT ABOUT THE CHILDREN?

Children fall under the principal applicant's visa status until the age of 21. Spouses and children receive H-4 or L-2 visas. E visa dependants receive the same designation as the principal alien endorsed as the dependant. Spouses and children may not work in the US without a visa that specifically authorises employment. Dependent status does not authorise employment. After age 21, children must obtain independent immigration status.

Many dependants are in university at the time they turn 21 years of age and may qualify for F-1 student status. Children with an F-1 student visa, with few exceptions, cannot work except for a one-year period of practical training. At some point the child will graduate. At that time, adult children must change from F-1 to another visa category, or return home.

Getting a visa of their own

Dependants over 21 years of age cannot work or stay in the US for the long term without getting married to a US citizen, or finding a job that leads to a visa. Most university graduates, if they can find a job requiring a university degree, will qualify for H-1B status. The H-1B visa holder must go through labour certification to qualify for a green card (see Chapter 9). This is often a two-year process and it is always costly.

Marriage of convenience is out of the question. First of all it is illegal. Then consider the fact that the foreign spouse is hostage to the US spouse until the green card arrives and possibly after. Those who are found out can be prohibited from coming to the US forever. As in most things, life is tough but it's tougher if you are stupid.

As a result, some parents obtain green cards before the children reach 21. The green card petition includes children under the age of 21. A green card permits children to remain in the US without parents, and to freely study and work in the US. State universities treat green card holders as residents eligible for the less costly resident tuition.

EXPLORING THE ALTERNATIVES

As you can see, there are several viable approaches to staffing a new company in the US. In most cases, you will choose the L-1A visa, but there are good reasons to explore the other alternatives.

8

Staffing an Existing US Business

Now that we have described how to staff a start-up enterprise, let's look at staffing existing businesses. This chapter discusses:

- Treaty trader or treaty investor E-1 and E-2

- L-1A Manager

- L-1B Specialised Knowledge

- H-1B Professional Visas

- H-2B Seasonal Workers or Labor Unavailable in the US.

CHOOSING THE CORRECT VISA

Each visa category presents advantages and disadvantages. Consuls generally process E visa petitions faster than the INS processes H and L visa petitions. L-1A visas work better than other categories in start-up situations. H-1B petitions require LCA disclosures. The LCA disclosure entails additional processing time and may disturb relations with US workers. L-1B visas tend to require detailed explanations of the applicant's benefit to US competitiveness, while L-1A visas tend to require detailed explanations of the company's organisation and the applicant's managerial duties.

The E-1/2 essential skill category requires the US company to train replacements. The H-2B category requires recruitment of US workers. H and L visas have maximum validity periods, while E visas may be extended indefinitely. On the other hand, H-1B, L-1A, L-1B and E visas all permit the applicant to work in the US while allowing dependants to live and attend school in America.

MANAGERS

Most L-1A or E manager petitions are straightforward. Companies hire an endless variety of managers and executives, including administrative managers, human resource managers, accounting managers, production managers, company officers, sales managers, *etc*. Simply put, managers tell other managers, supervisors and professionals what to do.

Problems arise when the so-called manager is actually a front line supervisor. Front line supervisors do not manage other managers, supervisors or professionals. INS often questions petitions for production managers, sales managers and other positions that are often non-managerial. In such cases be prepared to furnish detailed organisational charts of the position abroad and the proposed position in the US as well as payroll records.

Managers and executives working for an international organisation may qualify for L-1A Manager, E-1/2 Manager, or H-1B Manager serving in a professional capacity. Managers working for a treaty company that isn't part of an international organisation qualify for E-1/2 or H-1B. If the company isn't a treaty organisation or an international organisation, H-1B Professional status becomes the only choice. Treaty organisations or international organisations may pay managers from abroad. In such cases the US employer must remit payroll tax and income tax withholding to the IRS for wages earned in the US.

Managers may commute between foreign and American locations. If questioned, the manager must demonstrate that he performs managerial duties while in the US. It's not how much time the manager spends in the US, it's what the manager does while there.

Corporate organisation will either expand or limit your

choices. Assuming you have all three choices – H-1B, L-1A and E-1/2 – consider the following points.

Factors favouring E visas

- In most cases, consuls process visas faster than INS.

- E visa holders receive up to two-year stay periods every time they enter the US. An E visa holder entering the US on the last day of his visa may be admitted for up to two years beyond the visa expiration date.

- L or H visa holders will only be admitted for a period not longer than their visa validity date. Depending on the circumstances, the E visa may eliminate the need to file an extention petition with the INS.

- The E visa may theoretically be extended indefinitely, whereas the H visa is limited to six years and the L-1A visa is limited to seven years.

- If the company is replacing an E visa holder with a person serving the same position, use the E visa category for the replacement. By granting the E visa the first time the consul has already determined that the position qualifies.

Factors favouring H and L visas

- Consuls usually review the US employer's staffing history. Consuls generally resist granting E visas for more than one person per position. The INS only reviews the case in front of them, and usually doesn't review the entire company's staffing structure and visa history. For example, if you think there will be trouble justifying the need for more than one sales manager, use the L-1A or H-1B categories.

- Consuls tend to question E visa petitions for managers under 30 years of age. In such cases, if the manager also has a professional degree consider H-1B or L-1A.

- If your company frequently uses E visas and cannot demonstrate a declining ratio of foreign versus American workers, consider H and L visas for new positions.

Determining the correct visa is more of an art than a science. One must consider long-term staffing goals. If your company plans to rotate managers between the US and foreign offices, it's important to establish precedents with the INS and consuls for all possible categories.

If hiring a foreign manager is an infrequent or one-time situation, use the visa category that best suits the applicant's credentials and long-term goals. For example, if the applicant may ultimately want a green card and the US employer is part of an international organisation, use the E or L-1A categories. As you will see in the next chapter, changing to a green card from an H-1B visa can be difficult.

Unless you ultimately want a green card, there is little practical difference between any of these visa categories. Choose the category that facilitates staffing the US business in the quickest and smoothest way possible. Applicants often qualify for several visa categories, and it is important to match the job requirements and applicant's skills with the most appropriate category. The closer the match, the faster the processing.

H-1B VISAS

The H-1B visa is the preferable visa category for professionals. Professional positions include most jobs that require a baccalaureate or higher degree as a minimum requirement. These could include accountant, engineer, economist, teacher, scientist, market researcher, sales engineer, psychiatrist, dietician, forester, hotel manager, librarian, journalist, medical doctor, minister, nutritionist, pharmacist, sociologist, lawyer, veterinarian, vocational counsellor, fashion model, technical publications writer and social worker.

The H-1B visa category offers simplicity. If the job requires a professional and the applicant has the appropriate professional background, the visa will be approved. Although US workers must be notified of the impending H-1B petition, and the employer must attest that it solicited equally qualified US workers before hiring the foreign worker, there is no requirement to recruit or hire US workers. There is also no requirement that the applicant have experience in the job offered. Recent college graduates often qualify for H-1B status. On the downside, the notification procedure, Labor Conditions Attestation, though relatively simple, requires additional processing time.

H-1B petitions require:

- information about the applicant's professional abilities
- information about the employer's need for a professional to fill the offered position
- the applicant's resumé
- and their educational credentials.

The size of the employer makes little difference in clearly professional positions, such as engineers and accountants. Small companies often have trouble justifying the need for a professional to fill marketing and administrative positions. For example, a small company has little need for the permanent services of a market researcher. The INS might suspect that the 'market researcher' who holds an economics or marketing degree is really a salesman.

Small companies generally don't need professionals such as business administration degree holders to fill administrative positions. Most small business managers learn on the job. A baccalaureate degree is usually not a job requirement for the small company business administrator or manager. Large companies with complex management structures fare better in demonstrating the need for business administration, MBA or other business-related degree holders.

Virtually all H-1B applicants have a university degree. Because the law does not require prior work experience, the INS, particularly in the case of young applicants, often questions whether the proposed employment in the US requires the services of a professional. INS may ask for employment advertisements from peer companies that require a university degree for the position, as well as letters from peer companies stating that they believe the position requires a professional education. INS often requests an analysis of the applicant's university study and experience to demonstrate the applicant has the skills to fill the position.

Applicants without a university degree may also qualify for H1-B status. As a rule of thumb three years' work experience equates to one year of university study. Applicants who attended two-year college courses in computer science or related fields often successfully qualify for H-1B status. Applicants who failed to finish their liberal arts degree usually make hopeless cases. In any event the INS will require a professional credentials evaluator to determine whether the applicant's education and experience equates to a baccalaureate university course of study.

COMMON APPLICATIONS OF H-1 VISAS

Financial and business professionals

Foreign-owned companies often transfer financial and accounting professionals to oversee cost-containment, the purchase of raw materials or parts, preparation of financial reports for the home office, and general accounting and financial activities. Typically the transferee lacks managerial experience and the job in the US rarely contains a managerial component. The lack of managerial experience eliminates any managerial visa possibilities.

As finance-related skills are widely available in the US and usually don't aid US competitiveness, L-1B specialised knowledge or E-1/2 essential skill visas are not recommended for these employees. H-1B status for finance and accounting positions is recommended for four reasons:

- The work falls within established professional disciplines.

- The services of a professional are required to understand financial, accounting or procurement systems.

- The applicant generally has an appropriate university degree (finance, economics or business administration).

- There is no requirement to demonstrate a shortage of US workers or that US workers cannot perform the job.

A typical job description for an economist, accountant or financial officer might be as follows:

'Prepare financial reports, budgets, analyse operating results as compared to budget projections, coordinate home office and subsidiary accounting methods, monitor cost control, prepare and analyse forecasts for executive management, work with outside professionals regarding tax return preparation and financial reporting.'

ENGINEERS

We recommend H-1B visas for non-managerial engineers or scientists (mechanical, electrical and computer engineers, *etc*) because engineering is a recognised profession usually requiring a related university degree.

Sales engineers often pose difficult cases. Is the sales engineer a salesman or an engineer? Sales managers may qualify for L-1A or E visas; salesmen do not qualify for any visa category. The typical sales engineer holds an engineering-related university degree, works on product development and design, and provides technical support to customers. The sales engineer explains the product in layman's terms.

Companies that manufacture or sell complicated products in the US hire sales engineers to 'explain the product to the customer, provide technical support to company salesmen, interface with the customer's engineers and technicians, provide customer technical support, and, after warranty service, work with customers' engineers and technicians regarding product modification, and install and monitor maintenance programs'.

This job description describes sales activity. But the sales engineer also requires technical expertise and a theoretical understanding of the product's mechanics, hence the engineering background. A successful H-1B petition hinges on emphasising the technical aspects of the job. Stress the technical or professional understanding of the product required to make the sale, rather than the salesmanship angle.

Use H-1B when managerial visas are inappropriate and the applicant has a four-year degree relating to a professional discipline. Liberal arts degrees in such areas as literature, business administration, English or other languages are problematic because the degrees only tangentially relate to the job offered.

The H-1B category presents four disadvantages. The duration is limited to six years; it's difficult to go from H-1B to green card status because of the labour certification requirement; and the employer must go through the LCA procedure, and there is a $500 charge in addition to the normal filing fee to fund worker training, scholarships and INS operations. Therefore, use the H-1B visa category in the following circumstances:

- The corporate organisation makes the H-1B the only choice.

- If there are choices, use the H-1B if the applicant is young and has little experience and a qualifying BA degree.

SPECIALISED KNOWLEDGE AND ESSENTIAL SKILLS

Companies often transfer specialists who work with a
particular product, technology or process. Specialists may
qualify for four visa categories: E-1/2 **Essential Skill**, L-1B
Specialized Knowledge, H-1B **Professional**, or H-2B **Labor
Unavailable** in the US.

If the applicant earned a university degree related to his
speciality, we recommend H-1B. Such an applicant, for
example, would have a Bachelor of Science degree in
fisheries for a marine-products specialist, computer science
degree for a computer/software specialist, and a forestry
degree for a wood products specialist.

It is easier to prove that the university degree relates to
the applicant's speciality than to prove that the applicant's
skills are essential to the US enterprise (E visa), or an aid
to US competitiveness (L-1B). An H-1B visa works
because the applicant must use professional skills to
understand, modify or analyse a complex product,
technology or process.

If a specialist lacks a university degree but holds skills
unavailable in the US necessary to the company's success,
consider E-1 Essential Skills status. If the specialised skill
helps promote US trade or exports, the applicant may
qualify for L-1B Specialized Knowledge status. Since both
categories face equally intense scrutiny, choose the
category that best matches the facts of the case.

L-1B and E-1/2 essential skills refer to the same sorts of
skills but with a different emphasis. 'Essential skills' refers
to skills critical to the US company's success. In other
words, the success of a US business depends upon the
applicant's essential skills. Additionally, the essential skills
in question must be unavailable in the US. The US treaty
company must usually agree to train people to replace the
essential skills applicant.

For example, it's often impossible to effectively use
foreign machinery without the temporary services of a
technician who provides training and technical support.
American technicians are unfamiliar with the newly

introduced machinery, so the US treaty company must agree to train technicians from the US.

Specialised knowledge refers to skills or knowledge of the parent company's product or processes which must be transferred to the US subsidiary for increasing the subsidiary company's competitiveness. The emphasis is on helping US competitiveness, not the necessity or scarcity of the skill. Although the US produces many software engineers, the installation of the parent company's particular software in the US subsidiary may aid the US subsidiary's competitiveness in international markets.

Who can use L-1B and E Essential Skill visas?

There's an endless list of appropriate applications for the L-1B and E essential skills visas. In general, use this category for persons with technical skills who lack university degrees. Some points to remember:

- Use another category unless the applicant doesn't qualify as an international manager or have a professional degree. Professionals and managers may also hold specialised knowledge or essential skills.

- The consuls and INS scrutinise L-1 specialised knowledge cases and E essential skills cases more than managerial or professional cases.

- Use L-1 specialised knowledge when transferring knowledge which helps US competitiveness. The knowledge does not have to be secret or proprietary. On the other hand, if everyone has this knowledge how can it aid US competitiveness? A lot of companies make instant noodles, but not everyone's instant noodles taste the same. The knowledge that makes Company A's noodles taste different from its competitor's is specialised.

- Use E essential skill status when the emphasis is on training US labour to fill a skills shortage. The skill must be unavailable in the US and essential to the success of the business. Essential does not necessarily mean complicated. Marine products technicians hold essential skills due to a US skills shortage, not because of the complexity of processing fish.

- The drawback to the E essential skill category is that you may need to agree to train US workers to eliminate the need for an essential skill employee. Because of the training requirements, it's difficult to convince consuls to renew E essential skill visas. Although you can claim high turnover, or changes in technology prevented you from training a replacement, there is a limit to the consul's patience.

- The more esoteric or complicated the skill the easier the case. For example, it's easier to convince consuls or the INS that a nuclear physicist working on a new atom-smasher holds more essential skills or specialised knowledge than a noodle technician. In the case of the nuclear physicist, emphasise the complexity of the skill. In the case of the noodle technician, emphasise the contribution to local employment and the export trade.

- Time limits: Consuls issue E visas for up to five years. E visas may be renewed as long as you can convince the consul to issue the visa. There is no limit on extensions. The law limits L-1B visa validity to a total of five continuous years. After the five-year period the applicant must leave the US for a year before applying again.

The 'technicians' option

If the applicant fails to qualify for any other nonimmigrant status, consider the H-2B visa, which applies to skilled or unskilled labour unavailable in the area of intended employment. The key factor here is availability. It does not matter whether you import rocket scientists or ditch diggers as long as the labour is unavailable.

H-2B workers must work seasonally or fill a one-time need. Trainers coming to the US to teach American workers a procedure, such as a chef showing American cooks a new cuisine, fill a one-time need. Theoretically, the trainee takes over the position. This does not apply to child monitors or amahs, who fill a nonrecurring position. The child eventually grows up.

The employer must advertise the position, interview the job applicants, and convince the Department of Labor that none of the job applicants meets the *minimum* job requirements. The Department of Labor establishes minimum job requirements and acceptable salaries, and determines which job applicants to interview. If you succeed with the Department of Labor the job will be certified as available to foreign workers. Then you must petition the INS for visa approval.

The entire process takes between 90 and 120 days, and the H-2B visa lasts for one year. To extend the visa the entire process must be repeated.

RECRUITMENT DIFFICULTIES

If there is a choice, use the E-1 essential skill or L-1B specialized knowledge categories because they do not require recruitment. The recruitment process puts the employer in an awkward position. The employer hopes to prove that no qualified US workers exist, and often does that by finding reasons not to hire the people answering the job advertisements. Understandably, the jilted job applicants often complain to the Department of Labor. The cost of advertising and inconvenience of interviewing undesirable applicants often make the process distasteful.

OTHER H-2B APPLICATIONS

Use the H-2B visa when your employees fit into a category of workers who customarily use the H-2B visa, or there is no other choice. Sheep ranchers in Montana use H-2B visas for Basque shepherds. People who want to hire domestic help or someone to take care of their children use H-2B visas for nannies and amahs.

Restaurants sometimes use H-2B visas for chefs. Farmers use H-2A (agricultural) for farm workers. Manufacturers, when all else fails, use H-2B for technicians and trainers.

Using the H-2B visa for technical workers–marine products technicians

The marine products industry uses H-2B visas to send technicians to Alaska to process pollack, salmon, herring roe, surimi and other species of fish. The US suffers a shortage of marine products technicials qualified to service foreign markets. Japanese, Korean and Norwegian companies send hundreds of marine products technicians to Alaska on a seasonal basis. The technicians work on short-term contracts. There is a long history of negotiation in this industry, with the INS and Department of Labor on one side and the marine products industry in opposition.

The US packer wants to ensure that the product meets buyers' specifications before it reaches the market. The buyer who distributes the products abroad wants assurance that the product meets his market requirements. To meet contractual requirements, the buyer must send its technicians to each packing plant to render technical assistance and quality control. This is a perfect scenario for using H-2B visas.

Since there is no American market for most of the marine products exported to Japan, few qualified US workers exist. And since foreign technicians only work on short-term contracts, there is no sense in applying for long-term visas, such as E-1 essential skill or L-1B specialised knowledge. Employers may spread advertising and recruitment over many visas, as up to 50 technicians often apply at the same time. Advertising and recruitment costs can be prohibitive when applications are made for only a few technicians at a time. Finally, because of its long history of negotiation, the Department of Labor understands the need for foreign technicians and, to an extent, cooperates with the industry.

The marine products industry offers only one example of using the H-2B visa for technical workers. The same approach may be used for all sorts of non-degreed skilled labour, such as welders, machinists, electricians and more.

REVIEW OF GUIDELINES FOR SPECIALISTS

* All things being equal, use L-1B or E essential skills as opposed to H-2B.

* Use E essential skill or L-1B specialised knowledge for long-term technician employees. If an employee only works on a short-term basis, consider the H-2B category.

* Choosing between L-1B or E essential skill visas usually hinges on whether you feel the INS or a consul is more receptive to supporting your situation.

* Always apply for the maximum number of H-2B positions. You may have to hire US workers. You want to make sure US workers can be hired while still bringing in your minimum requirement of foreign employees.

* To show good faith in recruiting American workers, provide the Department of Labor with plans to eliminate dependence on foreign workers.

* Remember, cooperate with the Department of Labor during the H-2B process, and don't get frustrated.

BALANCING FOREIGN AND US EMPLOYMENT

The US subsidiary or branch office of a foreign company often employs more alien workers than Americans. Many companies prefer to use their own employees to make large purchases, handle money, or ensure quality control. These factors combine to limit the number of American workers above the secretarial level in the US operation.

Consulates often notice the high ratio of foreign professional workers and strongly suggest hiring more local employees. For immigration purposes, green card holders are US workers. Many companies solve the consular-imposed problem by obtaining green cards for managerial staff.

PREVENTING THE DISCRIMINATION LAWSUIT

Discrimination and sexual harassment law suits most often arise in connection with terminating the employee. The US is a litigious society. Foreign workers, unfortunately, are quick to learn our bad habits.

US workers must be paid the same salary as the foreign worker for the same work. Foreign transferees are often compensated for their overseas work by receiving bonuses paid from abroad as well as enhanced company benefits and housing allowances.

When evaluating the wage discrimination issue, pay close attention to the respective compensation and promotional packages offered to foreign and American workers. If the foreign worker receives a higher compensation package than the US worker for the same work, be prepared to face a lawsuit. Also expect litigation if the US employee does not progress through the company ranks at the same rate as the equally qualified foreign worker. The federal Equal Employment Opportunity Commission often supports such lawsuits in order to uphold anti-discrimination laws.

Branch offices worry less about these types of concerns. Most FCN and BIT treaties, in so many words, give branch offices the right to discriminate in favour of treaty nationals holding E-1 or E-2 visas. There is no right to discriminate in favour of H and L visa holders working for a treaty company. The US Supreme Court made that decision and it's still the law, though it is currently under attack. Given the correct facts, this exception to the civil rights laws may change. This is one of the few advantages of operating as a branch office.

The law requires all employers to provide equal pay for equal work. Equal pay for equal work means general equality of the net result, not identical benefit and compensation packages. Equal pay for equal work, full disclosure of job duties and compensation packages, as well as general fairness, will solve most problems between foreign and local staff members.

Finally, beware of sexual harassment law suits. Obviously, touching, direct sexual advances and leering constitute sexual harassment. Higher ranking employees imposing themselves on lower ranking employees, as well as off-colour jokes about either sex may constitute sexual harassment. Most insurance companies do not insure corporate officers against sexual harassment law suits. There's only one cure, behave!

9

Five Ways to Obtain a Green Card

Foreign companies move employees to America to staff a business. Foreign nationals, often, establish a US business as a vehicle for permanently moving their families to the US. Among the more common reasons for moving to the US are concerns for safety, fear of instability or unpredictability with the home country's government, children's schooling, quality of life, and retirement.

Investors who merely wish to invest or own property in the US needn't read any more of this chapter. Anyone can buy property, open a bank account, operate a business, or own a house in the US without a visa. Some nations, not the US, permit self-supporting people to retire or reside indefinitely in their country. Although there are proposals in Congress for a retirement visa, for now, people who wish to live, work or retire in the US require a visa.

Moving to a strange country involves planning and patience. Many people require several years to make the transition of living comfortably in the US. People commonly work in the home country during the transition period, while the children or family members live in America. Everyone who decides to move to America must resolve unique problems. Yet the goal of permanent US residence remains the same. Several visa strategies accomplish this same result:

- Family Class: Application through a close family member.

- Investment in the US.

- Application on the basis of extraordinary skills.

- The Two-Step: Managerial transfer.

- Labor Certification: US employer proves that no US workers can fill your job.

UNDERSTANDING GENERAL CONCEPTS

The 'green card' is evidence of Lawful Permanent Residence status. The credit card-sized green card, officially called an Alien Registration Card, although originally green, turned blue, then pink. Despite the changes in colour the green card retained its original name.

Any green card application requires three basic steps:

1. Unless exempted, all employee-based permanent residence applicants must first prove that no American citizens meet the minimum job requirements ('labour certification'). We discuss the following exemptions: exceptional skills, national interest waiver, investment or employment creation, and multinational manager. Family-class green card applicants do not need labour certification.

2. Secondly, the applicant must file an immigrant visa petition with the INS on the prescribed form.

3. Finally, upon petition approval the applicant must file documents for the green card interview.

Petitioning for permanent residence status

The green card petition requests classification as a particular category of permanent residence. Family-class applicants use Form I-130, employment class applicants use Form I-140, and investors use Form I-526. The petition and supporting documents are filed at an INS Regional Processing Center. The applicant then must wait for the result. The INS will either issue an approval letter, deny the application, or ask for more information. The processing period varies from 90 to 180 days. Upon petition approval, assuming a visa is available, applicants may proceed to the next step, the interview.

Green card petitions include spouses and children under age 21, as of the approval date of the adjustment of status or consular application. For example, your child turns 21 on 1 March 1999 and you filed the adjustment of status documents on 1 December 1999. If the INS approves the adjustment of status to permanent residence on 2 March 1999, the 21-year-old child will not qualify.

Children over 21 are eligible for second-family preferences. Due to the quota wait, now approximately two years, the child must obtain another visa status through employment or as a student to remain in the USA.

Waiting for visa availability

In order to interview, the INS must approve the petition and a visa must be available. Petitioners often encounter a waiting period. This 'quota wait' occurs between the petition filing date and the date a visa becomes available.

The US quota system seeks to limit annual permanent residence visas to approximately 480,000 family class, 140,000 employment class, 10,000 special immigrants (such as investors), and 55,000 diversity class (called lottery) divided among the various permanent residence categories. The quota exempts immediate relatives, spouses, parents and children of US citizens who may interview immediately after visa approval.

The visa allocation formula annually grants each country or group of countries approximately 25,000 visas. Quota waits occur when a country uses its annual visa allotments plus unused visas from other countries. For example, high demand from countries such as Korea, China, India and Mexico has caused a minimum nine-year quota wait for brothers and sisters of US citizens of these origins. On the other hand, most employment-based categories experience no quota wait.

The waiting period begins on the date (called the 'priority date') of filing the petition with the INS or

Department of Labor, as the case may be. Persons holding a current priority date may file for the interview. The State Department publishes *The Visa Bulletin*, which lists current priority dates by category once a month. Because visa demand varies by country and visa category, there is no way to accurately predict the movement of priority dates.

Going on the dole
Green card holders are ineligible for social security, national pension benefits, and Medicare benefits unless they have worked one day in each of 40 calendar quarters or ten years. Green card holders may qualify for social security disability benefits. The calendar quarters do not have to be consecutive. State governments may at their discretion offer green card holders some welfare benefits. Missing social security may not be too big a deal; it may not be around by the time many of us need it.

Guaranteeing you won't go on the dole
All family class green card applicants must be guaranteed by a US citizen or permanent resident. The guarantor must guarantee that the applicant will not be a public charge for three years. See Form I-864. Employment-based applicants have little problem because they have a job and an employer. Individuals often have problems with the guarantor requirements.

The guarantor, a US citizen or green card holder living in the USA, must prove an annual income of at least 1.5 times the poverty minimum, about $24,000 a year. Those without a guarantor, often lottery winners and spouses of green card holders or US citizens living abroad, are simply out of luck unless they can find an immigrant's aid organisation or surety who is willing to serve as a guarantor.

Getting sick without insurance
The US does not have a national health system for

persons under 62 years of age. Medicare is a national health system for those over 62 years of age. The US government determines the doctors' rates and acts as a single payor. All doctors must participate in the programme. There is no supplementary insurance and doctors may not charge more than the Medicare rates, even to willing customers.

As in the case of social security benefits, green card holders are ineligible for Medicare unless they work for 40 calendar quarters. Most green card holders must either pay for private health coverage or be prepared to fly home in case of serious illness.

BEING INTERVIEWED FOR PERMANENT RESIDENCE STATUS

The interview verifies eligibility for an immigration classification, and checks for grounds of exclusion from the US. Grounds for exclusion include criminal records, undesirable political affiliations, certain diseases, and lack of financial support. You may have your interview with the INS at an office nearest your US residence, or you may attend an interview with the US Consulate nearest your place of foreign residence. The INS process is called an **Adjustment of Status to Permanent Residence**. The consular process is called **Application for Immigrant Visa and Alien Registration**. Both processes achieve the same ultimate results.

The term 'Adjust Status to Permanent Residence' refers to the procedures required to change from a nonimmigrant status to a permanent resident. No aliens except for immediate relatives may be interviewed in the US without being of legal status. Aliens in illegal status must be interviewed at a Consulate abroad.

The INS and consulates require the same basic information and tend to ask the same interview questions. In choosing whether to be interviewed with the INS or a Consulate, consider local processing times, local enforcement policies and convenience, which vary among INS offices and consular posts.

CHOOSING BETWEEN ADJUSTMENT OF STATUS AND CONSULAR PROCESSING

Consular processing is usually faster, four to six months compared with a year or so, and procedurally more convenient than INS processing. One may not travel during the adjustment of status processing period without applying for special travel permission, **advance parole**. If one travels without advance parole, the INS may deem the adjustment of status petition abandoned. The applicant may be denied admission to the US or have to refile and start the adjustment of status proceedings from the beginning.

Advance parole requires a separate petition and filing fee, takes 30–60 days to process, and is usually valid for six months. Although the advance parole provides for multiple entries to the US during its validity period, the adjustment of status proceedings often takes over a year. If you intend to travel frequently it's often more convenient to have the interview with a Consulate abroad.

People fearing strict consular enforcement often choose to have their interview with the INS. If problems arise they may remain in the US while solving the problem. If problems occur during a consular interview, you must usually remain abroad until they are resolved. Also, appeals of an INS decision can be made to an independent court. If a consul denies an application the matter must be resolved with the US State Department. No independent judges review consular decisions.

WORKING DURING THE ADJUSTMENT OF STATUS PROCESSING

Adjustment of status applicants may simultaneously apply for employment authorisation. The applicant should receive a laminated card authorising employment within 30–60 days of applying.

Many employment-based green card applicants want to change jobs or be self-employed as soon as they get their green card. Although the employment authorisation card permits you to work for any employer, the petitioning employer and employee must intend a permanent, or at least long-term, employment relationship. If the INS were to discover that the employee had no intention of working for the petitioning employer, it could revoke the green card. Employees should work for the petitioning employer at least during the adjustment of status processing period and for a long enough time beyond to show good faith.

GREEN CARD CATEGORIES

Let's examine the various approaches to obtaining a green card, and explore the easiest options first.

Pursuing the easiest method first – family class

Family class petitions require proof of a qualifying relationship. Qualifying relationships include:

- *Immediate relative*: Parents and spouses of US citizens.

- *1st preference*: Unmarried children of US citizens.

- *2nd preference*: Spouses and unmarried children of permanent residents (unmarried children under 21 [2A] have priority over unmarried children over 21 [2B].

- *3rd preference*: Married children of US citizens.

- *4th preference*: Brothers and sisters of adult US citizens.

'Family class' merely requires proof of the qualifying family relationship. Most people do not use lawyers for family class cases, except for convenience or in the case of missing or nonexistent records. In most cases, if you can't prove that your mother is your mother, there is a problem no lawyer can solve. You may want to consult with an expert to guide you through the filing and interview procedures, help you organise important evidence and assist with timing.

Petitioning for family class status

The petition (Form I-130) generally requires proof of the US status of a relative and proof of relationship with that relative. To prove the required family relationship, attach the applicant's and sponsor's birth certificates, and provide proof of the sponsor's US citizenship or permanent resident status. The instructions on the I-130 Form suggest appropriate supporting documents and explain the filing procedures.

PLANNING FOR THE QUOTA WAITING PERIOD

The quota waiting period – the period beginning after visa approval and ending with visa availability – presents the biggest obstacle in family class cases, since it may cause several years of separation from family members. Adult siblings of US citizens usually work or manage businesses during the waiting period. Spouses and parents of American citizens experience no quota wait. The most common problem concerns spouses and children of green card holders.

A typical scenario: A husband with a green card marries a foreigner. The husband files for a green card and the INS approves a second preference petition for the new wife. A two-year quota wait is projected. The wife has no visa status other than a tourist visa.

What does this couple do during the quota waiting period? If the wife wants to live in the US with her husband, rather than merely visiting him, she will need independent visa status. Two choices should be examined here. The wife may find a job that leads to an independent visa, such as H-1B or E, or attend school on an F-1 visa. If neither of these visas can be arranged, the wife can only have short-term visits with her husband.

Depending on nationality, one may visit the US on visa waiver or with a B-2 tourist visa. Since visa waiver limits the visit to 90 days with no extensions, most spouses prefer a B-2 visa. As a rule, consuls do not issue B-2 visas to foreign spouses coming to the US to visit their American mates. If possible, apply for the B-2 visa before marrying.

Negotiating the waiting period with a B-2 visa

Most B-2 visas allow multiple entries over a five-year period. The INS usually admits B-2 visa holders for six months, and it's relatively easy to extend for an additional six months. But subsequent extensions are difficult. Plan on returning home after the one-year period. The second preference waiting period for spouses of green card holders is approximately two years. The B-2 visa method usually covers one of the two years.

Aliens cannot come to the US on a temporary visa when they intend to live permanently in the country. The INS generally assumes that a wife coming to visit her husband or vice versa intends to live with the spouse. The chances of entering the US may depend upon convincing an INS inspector that the visit is truly temporary.

It is easier to demonstrate intentions for *temporary* visits to the US if you have a job, family and property in your home country. For obvious reasons, the longer you stay home between trips the more clear it is that there are meaningful ties to your home country. Factors which prove an intention to return home after a short visit include a job or business in the home country, a residence, family, and proof that you've returned home after previous US visits.

Be honest, prepare supporting evidence, and make sure the INS appreciates the applicant's knowledge and understanding of the rules. Under the Summary Removal rules an INS officer may deny entry and prohibit future entries for five years if the officer believes that the applicant for entry misrepresented material facts. There's no hearing, no appeal, and no recourse other than to file a waiver of the grounds of exclusion with a consulate abroad. Waiver processing takes several months and, worse than that, requires consent of the Consul and the INS, thus reducing the chances of approval. The moral of the story is, whatever you do, don't lie!

The V visa.

The new V visa permits persons with an approved I-130 preference petition to join their US green card spouse if they have been waiting three or more years from the approval date of the I-130 preference petition. The V visa permits the applicant to work in the US and remain in the US with rights to travel until the quota becomes available. This means the maximum period of separation for those who marry a US permanent resident is three years plus the I-130 and V visa processing time.

Negotiating the quota waiting period by finding a job

Holders of university degrees may seek a sponsoring employer and explore the filing of an H-1B petition. If the spouse finds an employer of the same nationality qualified for E visa status, consider an E visa. Visa waiver or B-2 visa holders may legally look for jobs in the US. B-2 visa holders may find a job and change status in the US.

Many people change from B-2 to H-1B or E visa status and wait in the US, without leaving, until the green card is available. Since visa waiver holders may not change to another nonimmigrant status in the US after finding employment, they must obtain INS approval and return home to apply for the visa. All nonimmigrant visa applicants must disclose the green card applications submitted on their behalf. The INS cannot deny nonimmigrant work visa petitions solely because of a pending green card application.

Negotiating the quota waiting period as a student

Some spouses go to school as F-1 students. This option works for those who intend to go to school or want to continue school but need a compelling reason to do so.

Only serious students need apply, as a full course load must be maintained in order to keep the F-1 visa.

Summary
If the quota waiting period separates a foreign family member from a US relative, there are four choices:

- waiting at home
- visiting the US
- finding an American job and changing to a nonimmigrant work visa
- or going to school and changing to F-1 status.

In all cases you must be able to prove your intention to return home at the end of the temporary stay, in spite of a pending green card petition.

INVESTING IN AMERICA FOR A GREEN CARD

The US, like Canada, Australia, New Zealand and other countries, has an immigrant investor programme. The US requires an investment of $1,000,000 in a trade or business, and employment of ten full-time persons. The American programme is officially called the Employment Creation Aliens Program, or more commonly, the Investor Visa. The programme reduces the investment amount to $500,000 for rural or high-unemployment areas.

The US programme began in 1990. One of our first immigrant investor cases involved a mother and her two daughters, each of whom purchased 16.66 per cent of a construction company and large shopping mall. The husband had given the mother and each daughter $1,000,000, a total of $3,000,000, in a divorce settlement. The funds came from a US bank account. Although the mother and daughters served on the company's board of directors, they had no active roles in management. The project employed about 45 people, some on a part-time basis. This case satisfied the regulatory requirements and was duly approved.

Employee criteria

Any trade or business that employs at least ten persons per investor qualifies for this programme. You may start a business, buy a business, or invest in an existing commercial concern. The investment must increase the capital or employment of an existing business by at least 140 per cent. The people in the example above invested in an existing business.

Immigrant investors may hold minority interests in the business. Although investors must play a role in management, the regulations deem limited partners or members of the board of directors as active participants in management. As long as the business employs at least ten persons per investor, it may accept as many investors who make the required investment.

A 'full-time employee' is defined as someone working at least 37.5 hours per week, but employers may combine part-time employees to satisfy the definition. Twenty people who work 18.75 hours each equals ten employees. Independent contractors, such as trades people and cleaning service personnel, do not count as employees. Employees may not be immediate family members of the investor, but must be US citizens or green card holders.

PAYING BY CASH OR CREDIT

The law permits instalment payments of the required investment amount. Many investment programmes offer instalment payment plans or provide unsecured financing. INS does its best to deny petitions where the investment amount is paid in anything but one lump sum at the time of green card approval. Loans must be secured by the investor's assets. The investment amount may be placed in an escrow or trust account, provided the trust agreement states that the funds will be released to the business or target investment upon green card approval.

Investment fund sources

Investment funds may come from any legal foreign or US source, including gifts and divorce settlements. Applicants must be prepared to show the source of their investment funds. Corporate investors may not designate an employee or shareholder to receive the green card. Whoever receives the visa must make the investment. Borrowed investment funds qualify as long as the borrowed funds are secured by the assets of applicant but not the target US business. For example, investors may borrow against a home and use the loan proceeds to buy a business qualifying for the investor visa.

Business plan

The INS application, Form I-526, must include a business plan which details the application of funds to the target investment and demonstrates that the target business will support at least ten employees. The business plan should contain the level of detail one would provide a bank with to secure a commercial loan.

Investors have two years to make the investment and hire ten employees. The INS grants a conditional green card upon the initial investment, and two years later issues an unrestricted green card upon verification of the required employees and capital. There is no requirement to continue the investment beyond the two-year period.

Applicant suitability

Unlike Canada, Australia and New Zealand the US does not have investor suitability standards or a points system. There are no language or business experience requirements. The US investor must only prove the legal source of his investment capital.

Proving a legal source of funds may not be so simple.

The INS often denies petitions where the investor's tax returns do not show sufficient gross income over a five-year period to demonstrate how someone could accumulate the required investment amount. In such cases, proof of sales of assets, inheritance, loans or gifts may suffice.

THE REGIONAL CENTRE PROGRAMME

The ten employee requirement deters most investors. To encourage immigrant investors, the INS, in 1994, devised a slightly different scheme. Now immigrant investors may invest in INS-approved funds called **regional centres**. The regional centres are any project, private or public, that promotes US employment and exports in a particular region of the US.

The regional centre programme permits those who have money, but do not want to manage a US business and hire US workers, to obtain green cards. In this programme the promoter makes a proposal to the INS in Washington, D.C. to develop a region or area. If the INS believes the proposal will benefit a regional economy and shows potential for providing significant employment opportunities, the project will be designated a regional centre. With INS approval in hand, the promoter forms a limited partnership or corporation to raise money for specific projects.

Foreign investors may apply for green cards upon depositing their investment capital into an independent bank trust or escrow account. The investor's funds must be released to the closing agent for the designated project immediately upon visa approval.

Investors in a regional centre do not have to prove the business will employ ten persons. Instead, the regional centre may rely on government for its particular projects. For example, a regional centre proposing to develop an air cargo facility may rely on the indirect employment created by the air cargo facility to satisfy the ten-employee require-ment. Indirect employment includes direct employment plus jobs such as service industries that rely on the regional centre. If the job multiplier statistics demonstrate the regional centre will create 500 direct and indirect jobs, the regional centre may seek 50 investors. Most state economic development agencies provide job multiplier statistics.

Except for employment creation, regional centres must follow the same rules as those for the immigrant investor programme in the employment creation criteria.

Who manages regional centres?
Individuals, corporations and government agencies are eligible to manage regional centre projects. Local governments were responsible for sponsoring two of the first seven funds. Our law firm has established several privately-managed funds. Since government can also mismanage money, don't be comforted by its sponsorship of a fund.

For obvious reasons, very few people used the immigrant investor programme at the $1,000,000 level. Regional centres located in rural or high-unemployment areas, *ie* the $500,000 investments, are becoming popular. Agents representing several Immigrant Investment companies around the world offer a variety of regional centre investment opportunities. We carefully monitor regional centre activity, but because of rapid changes we did not publish activity lists in this book.

Some pitfalls with the immigrant investor category
Investment immigration is controversial. Although the emphasis is on investment, some people see nothing more than the privileged rich buying into their country. The immigration departments of Canada, US, New Zealand and Australia have at one time or another suspended their programmes, delayed processing petitions, or changed rules without notice. Successful investors put up with the uncertainty. Patience generally prevails.

If the investment fails within the two-year conditional green card period, investors could lose their money and green cards. The INS has no plan to deal with this unfortunate possibility.

Who should apply under the immigrant investor programme

If you want to own and operate a business that requires at least $500,000 capital and ten employees, the immigrant investor programme is for you. Otherwise, first investigate whether you qualify for a visa category that doesn't require at least $500,000 capital. If not, then consider the regional centre programme because it does not have the ten employee requirement.

The regional centre programme has been most often used by:

- Retirees who want to reside permanently in the US without working. You may not live in the US, whether or not you work, without a permanent residence visa. Typically, visits to the vacation home increase in duration to the point where the immigration inspector determines you live in the US and need a green card. At that point you have a home that you can't use without a green card.

- Parents who want green cards for their children so that they can attend US public schools without paying tuition, or attend lower-cost state universities (foreign students may only attend US public high schools for 12 months without paying tuition).

- Young people of means who want to start life in America.

- Non-citizens who wish to bring their parents to the US permanently.

- People of both sexes who, rather than risk embarrassing families, buy green cards for their lovers, who are happy living in the US while the sponsor enjoys reduced risks.

SUMMARISING THE IMMIGRANT INVESTMENT CATEGORY

The immigrant investment category provides the fastest, most expensive and safest way to get a green card. Investors may be assured of getting the visa before their funds are committed to the investment because capital may remain in a trust account until visa approval. E and L visa applicants must commit funds to the investment before filing their visa petition.

The biggest disadvantage to the immigrant investor programme, aside from the costs, is that immigrant investors receive a two-year conditional green card. The INS verifies the bona fides of the regional centre investment at the end of the two-year period. What happens if INS changes the rules mid-stream? What happens if the investment fails? In the first instance you go to court. In the second instance nobody knows because it hasn't happened yet.

RETIRING IN AMERICA: 'THE TWO-STEP' METHOD FOR MANAGERS, EXECUTIVES AND ENTREPRENEURS

As the fastest and easiest method for business people to obtain green cards, the **Two-Step method** permits international managers and executives to apply for green cards without labour certification. The exemption from labour certification saves considerable time and expense. The Two-Step works for managerial/executive transferees working for established international organisations, as well as for the small business people who create an international organisation and transfer themselves to manage the US operation.

Step 1 refers to transferring in a managerial capacity to the US within an international organisation. This requires establishing a US business qualifying as an L-1 international organisation, or using an existing L-1 international organisation and obtaining a nonimmigrant work visa as a managerial transfer.

The applicant must have worked in a managerial or executive capacity on the foreign side of the international organisation for one of the three years prior to the transfer to the US branch, subsidiary or affiliate of the foreign employer in a managerial or executive capacity.

Step 2 refers to the green card procedures, which may occur at any time after the US employer has been doing business for one year.

The Two-Step applies to international managers and executives regardless of visa type. Therefore, managers and executives may use H-1B, E-1/2 pr H-1B visas. The exemption from labour certification focuses on transfer in a managerial capacity within an international organisation, not the particular visa used to effect the transfer.

A common scenario

Let's look at how the Two-Step might work for an individual. A 'Mr Smith' owns an electric motor parts trading company in a foreign country. He wants his children to receive an American education, and his wife wants to live in the US with the children while they attend school. The Smiths ultimately want to retire in the US, so Mr Smith needs a long-term visa strategy for the entire family.

The first step

Mr Smith establishes a US subsidiary company and secures an office. He then applies for an L-1A visa to manage the new American company during the start-up phase. Smith's wife and children receive L-2 visas as dependants, thus allowing them to attend school. Mrs Smith may live with the children, but is not allowed to work. The L-1A must be extended after the first year. Managers of start-up companies must establish the company within one year. Mr Smith applies for and receives a three-year extension.

The second step
Immediately after the extension approval, Mr Smith applies for a green card as an 'International Manager or Executive'. Upon green card approval, he submits documents for the family's interview. If all goes well Mr Smith will receive a temporary green card within eight to 12 months of his petition, and he will receive a permanent green card about four months later. Within two years after arriving in America, Mr Smith, his wife and their children under 21 years of age will have green cards.

If Mr Smith transfers to a company established in the US for at least one year he may immediately apply for a green card. The exemption from labour certification depends upon managerial/executive transfer within an international organisation that has been doing business in the US for at least one year. The applicant needn't work in the US for one year. Theoretically, the applicant could apply from abroad as long as the international organisation conducted business in the US for one year, as the one-year period refers to the employer, not the applicant.

DETAILS OF THE TWO-STEP PROCESS

Step 1: Establish the US business/managerial transfer with a nonimmigrant work visa

Establishing a US subsidiary
Establishing a company means:

- incorporating a business

- obtaining federal tax identification numbers

- finding a place of business

- and getting relevant licences.

For a variety of tax and legal reasons, we recommend establishing a US corporation rather than a US branch office. In most cases, the applicant should issue shares to the foreign employer, which becomes the parent company. The subsidiary company must either lease or buy a place of doing business. Do not operate from a personal residence because the INS will query it.

The US company may buy property, purchase a business, or start a new firm, and conduct any business as long as it requires the services of a manager or executive. As a general rule, the business must hire employees; a one-person operation does not require a manager. The business plan should require at least three or four employees.

Any business qualifies for the Two-Step: real estate investment, import/export trader, merchant, manufacturer, restaurant manager or manager of a group of professionals. In fact, the US trade or business may be unrelated to the foreign parent's line of business. The foreign parent could be a trading company, while the US subsidiary could be a real estate management firm.

Choosing a nonimmigrant work visa
For green card purposes, any nonimmigrant work visa suffices as long as you transfer to the US branch, subsidiary or affiliate of the foreign employer in a managerial capacity. Established companies generally use the L-1A or E-1/2 options. Although H-1B visa holders may also serve in a managerial capacity, we don't recommend using H-1B status as a stepping stone in the Two-Step process. Consider the time and effort required to convince the INS that the H-1B professional also serves in a managerial position. The INS would want a convincing explanation as to why a managerial visa was not used in the first place. Most start-up companies should use the L-1A visa. Examine all visa options. Just make sure to transfer to the US as a manager.

Factors such as the nature of the US business, nationality, convenience, and consular *vs* INS enforcement policies, determine whether application should be made for E-1, E-2 or L-1A status. The INS will grant an initial one-year validity period for L-1A start-up companies. At the end of the one-year period the INS requires proof of progress toward establishing the US business. Consuls often deny E visa status for start-up companies.

E or L managers may be paid from the foreign parent company and commute between the US office and overseas locations. Two-Step managers may work part-time in the US. However, Two-Step managers must prove they exercise managerial control over the US business. Proof of managerial control includes authority to sign company documents, a history of reviewing company operations, management memoranda, minutes of management decisions, contract negotiation, hiring and firing, and budgetary authority.

Step 2: One year of doing business, multinational manager green card

Apply for the green card as a first preference multinational manager any time after the US company has been doing business in the US for one year.

'Doing business' means:

• regularly and systematically providing goods and services to customers.

The INS verifies gross sales, employment and business activity. Remember that most managers must hire subordinate employees to prove service in a managerial capacity. Persons managing a function or a division of a large company, *ie* a regional sales manager, do not need subordinate employees. This exception to the employee requirement does not help many small business applicants.

The 'one year of doing business' requirement means that the company did business in the US for a year. It does not mean that the individual, the transferee, worked in the US for a year. In other words, the applicant's foreign company can buy an established US business with a multi-year operating history. Since the US business operated for over one year, it means immediate transfer of the person to the new US subsidiary as a first preference multinational manager, skipping the first step of the Two-Step.

Beware of the many unscrupulous operators, principally in Pakistan, India, Taiwan, Korea, and China, who offer ready-made businesses for sale to those wishing to eliminate the first step of the Two-Step. Before joining such a scheme consider the Consul's surprise when he sees that a substantial manufacturing company needs a manager for its newly purchased dry cleaning franchise in New York.

ANOTHER TWO-STEP APPROACH

Green cards for corporate executives or managers and established organisations

Corporate executives and managers for established international organisations use the same Two-Step process as individual businessmen, but they benefit from a ready-made international organisation. Individual business people must create their own international organisation.

As a rule, an employer transfers a manager to a US member of the international organisation using an L-1 or E-1/2 visa. In the typical situation the manager worked in a managerial capacity for a member of the international organisation for one of the three years prior to being transferred to the US. The American operation has been doing business for more than one year prior to the transfer. This type of manager may apply for a green card immediately upon arrival in the US. Theoretically, the manager could apply for a green card before transfer while working for the parent company abroad.

Benefits for children and retirement
Many people seek green cards because their children want to attend an American university or they plan to retire in the US. Dependent children need a separate visa to remain in the US after the age of 21, usually F-1 student or a nonimmigrant work visa. At retirement, an executive or manager will no longer be an employee of an

international organisation. Upon retirement he must apply for a green card through investment, skills or family ties types of petitions. It's easier to obtain a green card as a multinational manager because of the exemption from labour certification.

Children under age 21 may simultaneously obtain green cards through parents as well as find a job after graduation without having to apply for a work visa. As a permanent US resident, the child may qualify for lower-cost resident tuition at state universities (private universities usually charge the same expensive tuition to all students). The savings in state university tuition for one child more than pay for any immigration legal fees, and is one of the better investments you can make.

Employer's point of view
Many employers resist employees' green card applications since green card holders may work anywhere they choose. After all, why go through the time and expense of a green card application only to lose an employee after they receive the green card? Conversely, nonimmigrant visa holders may only work for the sponsoring employer.

The law requires the employer to intend to hire the applicant permanently and the applicant to intend to work permanently for the petitioning employer. Thanks to President Lincoln, employers cannot force employees to work for them and it is virtually impossible to prove preconceived intent to leave the employer upon green card approval. Thus petitioning employers always risk losing their prize recruit to the competition the minute the green card is in hand.

While there is no perfect solution to this problem, many employers withhold the legal fees from the employee's salary for a period of several years to at least ensure they don't lose the legal fees and the employee. Some employers simply make the applicant pay for the green card legal fees. The latter approach almost ensures the loss of the employee because the employee feels he paid for his freedom.

Most middle-aged green card applicants worked their entire careers for a single corporate group, and it is difficult to find an equivalent job in the US. The middle-aged applicant usually won't move to a new company in a foreign land at the middle or end of their careers. Most want to spend more time on the golf course or in other leisure activities rather than undergo a mid-life career change. Those new to the corporate group pose a greater risk of using the employer to obtain a green card and then leaving.

Foreign-owned US employers may benefit when an executive or manager obtains a green card. Employers must file an Embassy Annual Report for E visa purposes, listing US and foreign workers and their positions. The embassy uses this report to monitor how many E visas it will grant for particular positions. Green card holders count as American workers and may free up a new E visa position.

TIMING AND PROCEDURE

Nonimmigrant work visa (Step 1)
File L-1A petitions at an INS regional centre. File E visa petitions at a consul or regional processing centre. INS filings require Form 129 and an L or E Supplement. Each consulate uses its own forms. Expect L-1A or E-1/2 visa processing to take about 120 days. E visa processing times depend on a particular consulate's policies. Unless buying or working for an existing business, you must wait until the US business can prove one year of active operation before applying for the green card. In Two-Step cases the green card application contains much of the same information as the L-1A or E visa petition.

Green card (Step 2)

File Form I-140 (Petition for Immigrant Worker) and supporting documents with the INS at a regional service centre. Allow up to six months for petition processing. Upon petition approval, file for a green card interview with the INS or consulate. Currently, multinational managers endure no quota waiting period.

ATTENDING THE GREEN CARD INTERVIEW

INS interview

Most Two-Step applicants have their interview with the INS because their families already live in the US. Choose whether to be interviewed with the INS or a consulate on the I-140 petition. To interview in the US, file the Adjustment of Status Package (Form I-485) and supporting documents with the INS. Most INS offices only conduct personal interviews for suspicious business-class cases. Otherwise, the INS merely reviews the adjustment of status documents, verifies police records, and usually mails the result and, hopefully, a temporary green card about a year after the filing. The temporary green card should be followed by the permanent green card within four months. Adjustment procedures vary among the INS district offices.

Consular interview

Alternatively, you may have your interview at a consulate. In the case of consular interviews, the INS sends files to a visa distribution centre in New Hampshire, called the National Visa Center (NVC). The NVC sends a biographical information package (called 'Packet 3') to the applicant and forwards the file to the correct consular post. The consulate contacts the applicant with interview details. Interview procedures vary among consular offices. Applicants generally receive a temporary green card at the time of the consular interview.

LOOKING AT THE GREEN CARD

The temporary green card, usually valid for six months, serves as a travel document and confers the same benefits as the permanent green card. The INS routinely extends temporary green cards if receipt of the permanent green card is delayed. Most interviewing INS offices issue the temporary green card on a letter-sized page or as an endorsed I-94 card.

The permanent green card, a plastic card manufactured in Arlington, Texas, contains the recipient's picture, fingerprint, date of birth, date of approval and other details.

Separate interviews for family members

Green card approval includes spouses and children under 21. Circumstances often cause families to be interviewed in different places. The principal alien – the one who received green card approval – must be interviewed first and obtain approval at either a consular post or INS office. The applicant must instruct the interviewing office to send the approval notice and file to wherever the rest of the family will be interviewed. The receiving post will notify the family of the interview dates. These procedures (called 'Following to Join') delay the process, and there is a risk of losing the file during transfer between interviewing offices.

TRAVELLING DURING THE INS INTERVIEW PROCESS

Two-Step business persons often make frequent trips abroad. The nonimmigrant visa automatically expires upon filing for adjustment of status with the INS, which means that adjustment applicants have no travel document between the date of filing the adjustment petition with the INS and receipt of the temporary green card. You therefore need 'advance parole' to travel abroad and return to the US. Advance parole serves as a travel document to enable travel abroad between the date of the filing adjustment of status forms with the INS and receipt of the temporary green card. The INS grants advance parole for business reasons or family emergencies. But note that procedures vary among INS offices. Those who interview before a consul need not worry about travel arrangements since, in most cases, the nonimmigrant visa usually remains valid until the interview date and receipt of the temporary green card.

The INS assumes that those who travel without advance parole have abandoned their adjustment of status petition. Offenders must either start again or be interviewed at an overseas consulate. Unfortunately, the INS enforces this nonsensical rule. It is much better to apply for advance parole than to fight the system.

AVOIDING COMMON PITFALLS

The lack of a foreign parent company destroys the required international organisation. Multinational managers must belong to an international organisation until receipt of the green card. Don't sell or close the foreign parent company after establishing a US subsidiary. If necessary, close the company after receiving the green card.

The Two-Step works because it qualifies managerial transfers within an international organisation for an exemption to labour certification. Caution: The person who owns or manages a US business as an individual, rather than through an international organisation, is ineligible for the exemption from labour certification.

Labour certification requires the employer to prove that no US workers meet the job's minimum requirements. If no qualified US workers apply, the US Department of Labor (DOL) will certify the position as available to foreign workers. This process may take up to two years.

To make matters worse, the DOL will not certify self-employed people because it assumes the self-employed worker will refuse to make their job available to US workers. What business owner will fire himself when a qualified US worker appears? Self-employed people who are not multinational managers cannot use the Two-Step process or obtain labour certification. Self-employed people should explore the investor visa, family class or exceptional skill categories.

CONCLUSION

At present, multinational managers experience no quota wait. Also, processing and procedural issues present few problems. Proposed cuts in employment-based immigration may create future quota waits. Prior to 1990 certain multinational managers experienced one- to two-year quota waits. Today is a good time to apply for a multinational manager green card. Indeed, the timing has never been better.

THOSE WITH EXTRAORDINARY ABILITIES IN SCIENCES, ARTS AND BUSINESS

People recognised internationally as being at the top of their field qualify for this category. Celebrities, distinguished crafts people, very successful business people, winners of Nobel Prizes, or people with broad recognition in their field qualify. Since the vast majority of readers will not qualify for this position, there is no need to elaborate on this type of visa petitioner beyond mentioning that it's available. Use Forms I-140 and MA-750A and B for this category.

QUALIFYING FOR NATIONAL INTEREST EXEMPTION

Persons with exceptional ability in business, the arts or sciences, and whose skills serve American national interest, qualify for the 'national interests' exemption from labour certification. A sponsoring employer is not necessary, and the petitioner may be self-employed.

'Exceptional' means well above average but not extraordinary, as in 'extraordinary ability'. Though the INS only vaguely defines the term 'national interest,' the lack of detail creates an opportunity. Rather than restricting the category to, say, scientists with doctoral degrees or engineers, the INS invites the applicant to make a proposal.

The INS focuses on whether the applicant's skills serve America's national, rather than regional, interests. The applicant's skills must also be 'significant'. Although the INS does not define 'significant', past history suggests that Montessori school teachers, origami paper folders and other holders of interesting but non-essential skills need not apply. Recently the INS was ridiculed in the national press for admitting poets nobody had ever heard of, wood carvers, the local Sushi chef and the like under the national interest waiver category.

Because of the INS's stricter standards, I recently refused to handle a file for a young up-and-coming film producer. No problem with the chap's films, but his case won't fly for lack of a pedigree. On the other hand scientists with publications in prestigious professional journals, inventors with patents, persons with demonstrated success in business or the arts may successfully apply.

Although most cases involve aliens with advanced education, parents or other obvious qualifications (such as participation in important projects), there are enough exceptions to recommend this category to anyone with demonstrable achievements who feels their skills contribute to the artistic, economic, business or scientific interests of the US.

Persons with unique knowledge of foreign markets often qualify. Businessmen with records for turning companies around may also qualify. (Interestingly, the INS holds that attorneys do not qualify for this category.)

Case study

As an example of the programme's flexibility, a salmon aquaculturist with no formal training, who developed some of the first fish foods used by salmon rearing farms, was qualified under this petition. This fish food leads me to an interesting diversion. According to my applicant, salmon rearing was heavily promoted by the Norwegian government to complement mink farming. Mink food consists of fish meal and grain. The new salmon food consisted of ground mink, sans fur which went into coats, which consists of fish and grain, as well as other additives. While all this makes ecological sense and won my applicant his green card, think about it next time you eat farm raised salmon. We stressed that salmon farming is necessary in the face of declining natural salmon runs.

Combining national interest exemption with labour certification

National interest exemption may be used in tandem with labour certification. Prospective employers should apply for this category, and simultaneously start the labour certification process. If the INS approves the national-interest petition, stop the labour certification process. If the petition is denied, continue with labour certification. The INS usually responds before one is committed beyond the point of no return in the labour certification process. Remember, labour certification is the last resort, and happiness is found when cancelling that application. Use Forms I-140 and MA-750A and B for this category.

THE LAST RESORT: LABOR CERTIFICATION

Those who don't qualify for an exemption from labour certification, read this section.

Getting the general outline

The applicant for labour certification must have an employer willing to advertise the position and prove to the Department of Labor (DOL) that no US worker meets the minimum job requirements. Quite often, after interviewing countless applicants all with credentials similar to a foreign application, the DOL determines that the foreigner is the only one who qualifies. The labour certification system tries to ensure jobs for US workers who can meet minimum job requirements.

An employer should be aware that this process may take over a year to complete. But the wait is worth it. Legal fees and the costs of advertising and other items range from $5,000 to $10,000 for the entire process, which includes labour certification, green card petition and interview.

In a typical case the applicant works for the prospective employer on an H-1B visa. Remember, H-1B visa holders generally don't qualify for the Two-Step. The US employer is pleased with the applicant's work and will go through the labour certification process to keep the employee. There is no requirement to work for the prospective US employer during the labour certification process; you may work abroad while the American employer files for your labour certification.

The DOL administers the labour certification process. It contracts with individual state job services or state departments of labour to conduct local labour recruitment and manage communications with the employer. The state job service recommends approval or disapproval to the DOL.

Job requirements and prevailing wage

Labour certification means that the US DOL has determined that no available US workers meet the minimum job requirements. Upon receipt of labour certification the applicant may petition for a visa through the INS. Every employment-based green card applicant must go through labour certification unless they qualify for one of the exemptions previously discussed.

The employer must prove that no American workers meet the minimum job requirements at the prevailing wage. The DOL determines the minimum job requirements and prevailing wage. The employer must advertise for and try to recruit persons meeting the minimum requirements, not the most qualified persons as in a normal situation.

The salary offered to the alien must equal or exceed the prevailing wage. The prevailing wage, based on DOL surveys, reflects the wage commonly paid for similar positions in the area of intended employment. Since most employers won't hire the worst person for the job, the prevailing wage actually represents the wage employers expect to pay to the person most suitable for the job.

The labour certification process forces employers to advertise for a person who meets the minimum job requirements, while offering the wages paid to the most qualified applicants. In a normal situation, employers hire the best person for the least money, not the worst person at the salary paid to the best people. Despite the bizarre logic of this process, most labour certification petitions are successful.

Labour certification forms

The labour certification form, ETA 750A, describes the job offer for recruitment purposes. It contains fill-in blocks for the General Job Description (Block 12), Education and Experience Requirements (Block 13), and Special Requirements (Block 14). ETA 750B contains blocks for the applicant's education and experience. Use this form to prove that the applicant meets the requirements of the job offered. There are different strategies for filling in the three key areas.

Steps in the labour certification process

The labour certification process may be divided into five steps:

1. Creating the job description.

2. State employment service approval of the job description.

3. Recuitment and advertising.

4. Approval by the US DOL.

5. Filing the Immigrant Visa petition with the INS.

Step 1: Creating the job description

The DOL recommends minimum job qualifications. These
may include the required years of experience, education
levels and specific job duties. Since the DOL bases job
requirements on US labour market surveys, American
workers usually qualify for a job defined by the DOL. The
DOL publishes the results of its surveys in the *Dictionary
of Occupational Titles* and other manuals.

The onus is on the employer to convince the
department that your position should include different
job-related requirements from the department's standards.
We generally start with the employer's actual job
requirements. If the DOL objects, attempt to justify the
employer's position based on the employer's past practices
and business necessity. The idea is to convince the DOL
that the employer based the job requirements on its
normal hiring policies and did not tailor the job
requirements to the applicant's skills and experience.

Sample Job Description Block 12

The following might be used as a job description for the
position of a marine products market researcher.

'Develop and maintain cost accounting system. Gather,
compile and analyse information from various fish
processing locations, unloading docks, freight
companies, *etc*. Determine costs of finished fish
products. Prepare entries to the general ledger accounts.
Supervise and document the flow of finished products.
Jointly prepare financial statements and perform
financial analyses. Provide detailed monthly profit/loss
information for each fish species and interpret the data
to recommend improvement and support for
managerial decisions. Responsibilities also include

accounts payable functions, inventory control and other accounting tasks assigned by the accounting manager. All duties performed on computer. Conduct detailed market analysis of China/Taiwan market. Develop, negotiate, service Chinese accounts. Large portion of duties performed with LOTUS software.'

Strategy
Provide as much detail as possible in a job description. Divide the job into its smallest components, as each component becomes a job requirement. The more components the greater the chance that US applicants will fail to meet a job requirement. Note the detail in the example cited.

All job requirements must have a relationship to performing the position. Be prepared to justify each job requirement. Ask yourself if you can perform the job without a particular requirement. If you can, the state Department of Labor, which reviews the job description, will strongly suggest elimination of that job requirement.

Education and Experience Block 13
The following might be used as education and experience for the marine products market researcher position.

Education. A Bachelor of Arts degree in accounting or economics required for this position.

Experience required. Job experience – 3 years; Related occupation: None.

Strategy
Employers who require more education and experience than suggested by the DOL must demonstrate the business necessity for the increased requirements. 'Business necessity' means proving that the requirement is essential to the employer's business.

For example, an employer requiring a Masters degree in accounting for a staff position, and five years' experience for an accountant, must establish a business reason for requiring the Masters degree, when most employers only require a Bachelor of Arts degree.

Because the Department of Labor bases educational and experience requirements on their job market surveys, it is difficult to deviate from their suggested requirements. Law courts tend to uphold the government job surveys. Without conducting your own job market survey, it's difficult to prove the inaccuracy of a DOL survey. On the other hand, the courts grant employers more latitude on the subject of actual job duties. For this reason it is preferable to argue about the job description and special requirements rather than the education and experience requirements.

A trap: experience gained with the petitioning employer

The applicant cannot use job-related experience gained with the petitioning employer to qualify for the job. For example, a company providing household goods moving services to Japanese customers wishes to hire a household goods movements supervisor. The applicant worked in Japan for two years as a supervisor in a household goods moving company, and worked for the prospective US employer for a year as a supervisor on an H-1B visa. The US employer normally requires three years' experience for supervisors. The applicant has two years' experience with another employer in Japan, and one year's experience with the US employer applying for the labour certification. The US employer may only require two years' experience as a supervisor, or it will exclude the applicant.

Special Requirements Block 14

The following might be used in the special requirements block for the position of marine products market researcher.

Special requirements. Minimum one year experience using LOTUS software system. Two years' professional or business experience in China. Must read, write and speak fluent Mandarin Chinese. Experience may be gained concurrently. Resumé and two references required.

Strategy

The special requirements distinguish this job from similar jobs. These requirements should be tailored to the employer's business requirements, not the applicant's credentials. For example, all accountants keep books and prepare financial statements. The accountant in the example also uses a foreign accounting system and does business in a foreign language. Employers must justify all special requirements as a business necessity. 'Business necessity' means that the requirement is essential to the employer's business success.

Justify language requirements by proving that the business must be conducted in the foreign language. For example, to prove that most of the customers speak Japanese, produce business correspondence and copies of phone bills. Use common sense to justify business necessity.

An accountant who audits both a US subsidiary and the Chinese parent company must know both American and Chinese financial reporting systems. A company that recently acquired a foreign technology may require a person with experience in that technology. A company hoping to open a foreign market may need a person experienced in that market. A company providing services to foreign particular customs and habits of the foreign nationals.

Step 2: State Job Service processing
Once satisfied with the job description, the employer must send it along with the application forms (ETA 750 A and B), a sample advertisement, and supporting documents

proving the applicant's qualifications to the State Job
Service. The advertisement recites the information
contained in blocks 12, 13 and 14. The job service will
normally assign a prevailing wage, assign a file number
(called a 'job order'), and ask the employer to justify
some of the job requirements.

The employer may have to justify special requirements.
For example, the employer may have to produce phone
bills and correspondence to prove it does business in a
foreign language. The job service may also question the
years of experience or the level of education required. If
the job offered combines aspects of two job descriptions,
justify why the two job descriptions were combined in one
position rather than simply hiring two people.

Most state job services are reasonable and, after some
negotiations, will reach agreement on the content of the
advertisement, job description, education and experience
and special requirements. State job service processing
times vary by state; expect the process to take at least a
year.

Step 3: Recruiting

After reaching agreement on the content of the job
description and other requirements, the state job service
will suggest which periodicals or magazines to use for
advertising the salary, job description and special
requirements of the position. The advertisement must run
for at least three days in a newspaper, usually including a
Sunday, or one issue of a monthly magazine. Prospective
applicants will send resumés to the job service or
employer. The job service establishes the recruiting
procedures, then it advises the employer which applicants
should be interviewed. The recruitment period lasts 30
days from the date the job service opens its job order.

Each interviewee must be notified (don't wait until the
end of the recruitment period to contact applicants) by
phone or letter, and be offered a personal interview. We
recommend sending a registered letter to each applicant
to show they were contacted. Employers must use normal

interviewing policy, and each interviewee should be given written reasons for rejection. The reasons must relate to the job requirements.

Do not let a lawyer handle the interview. (How would you feel if you went to a job interview and faced a company lawyer?) The DOL feels the same way, and will deny the case because the interview process was unfair.

A short cut
Employers who have recruited for the position, subject to labour certification, during the six months period prior to filing the labour certification petition with the state job service, may request expedited handling. Such employers must submit copies of advertisements and resumés of rejected applicants to show a record of diligent, but unsuccessful, recruitment for the petition. The state job service, if convinced of the bona fides of the employer's recruitment efforts, may agree to submit the file directly to the Department of Labor (see below) thus eliminating about six to nine months of haggling over job descriptions and recruitment.

Step 4: Department of Labor approval
After completing the recruitment process, the employer must prepare a written report detailing the results of each interview. The employer's report must show how each applicant failed to meet one or more of the job requirements. The employer sends the report to the job service, which will then recommend approval or denial to the US Department of Labor. Since the DOL generally relies on the job service's recommendation, it is best to reach agreement with the job service on all important issues before advertising and recruitment. The DOL will advise the employer of its decision. Approval is called a **Labor Certification**, meaning that the DOL has certified the job as being available to foreign workers. You may appeal denials and, quite often, the DOL lets you provide additional information to support a case.

Step 5: INS approval

With labour certification in hand you may file the immigrant petition with the INS. Use the same Form I-140 as most other employment-based petition. The filing and interview procedure is the same as for any other work-related immigrant visa petition. Generally, the INS approves cases with approved labour certifications.

Occasionally, the INS will question an employer's ability to pay the salary of the new employee or even question the existence of the employee. To prove the ability to pay the salary, the employer must furnish tax returns and financial statements to prove it can afford to hire the new employee at the wage stated on the labour certification application.

There are people who will create a job that doesn't exist for a relative or friend. The friend or relative obtains the green card, comes to the US and goes merrily on his or her way. INS often makes house calls to see if the employee actually exists.

I have had to deal with several cases of over-zealous INS investigators. Asians often use English names for everyday use, but use their Asian names for official purposes such as the visa application. An INS investigator visited a small trading company in Chinatown to inquire of a Mrs Wang, Hsiao-yun. Nobody knew this person at the company, except Nancy who claimed she's one and the same. The INS investigator, fresh from guarding our southern borders, was not a believer. I actually had to go to court to prove that Nancy and Mrs Wang were one and the same.

The priority date

The priority date for quota-waiting begins when the labour certification application is filed with the state job service. This means applicants are not penalised by the government's snail-paced handling of the paperwork, at least for quota purposes.

KEEPING YOUR GREEN CARD

After going through the time, effort, expense and heartache of obtaining a green card, did you know that it can be lost without its holder doing anything wrong? This does not include the rare instances when one forfeits a green card by committing a felony or serious crime.

Once in possession of a green card you must make the US your permanent residence, meaning that you must live in the US. The INS often questions green card holders at ports of entry and asks when they last visited the US. If you work abroad and make only one or two short trips to the US each year, the INS will assume that you live abroad unless proven otherwise. If you cannot prove that you live in the US, the INS inspector will confiscate your green card at the port of entry and you will have to go to court to get it back.

Green card holders must prove they live in the US, while nonimmigrant visa holders must prove they don't live in the US. Living in the US means making the US your primary and permanent residence. The INS considers factors such as having a residence, bank account, driver's licence, credit cards, regular bills and registered vehicle, and filing US income tax returns. You do not have to own a residence; you may rent or live with a relative. The INS looks at all the facts and makes a judgment call as there is no clear definition of living in the US. Instead, it is a matter of facts and circumstances.

Re-entry permits

If you need to leave the US for more than six months, we recommend applying for a Permit to Re-enter. The application for this permit affords you the opportunity to explain the reason for a temporary absence from the US, and to make a formal declaration that you do not intend to relinquish your permanent US residence. You must also agree to file US income tax returns. INS approval gives you permission to remain abroad for up to two years without risking loss of the green card.

File the Permit to Re-enter (Form I-131) at an appropriate INS regional processing centre. Expect a 120-day processing period. You must be in the US during the processing period. The INS will not give you permission to return to the US if you have already left. For those already abroad, there is a similar embassy procedure.

It is acceptable to explain that you were transferred abroad by your employer or that you have business abroad, and upon the conclusion of your assignment you intend to return to the US.

The re-entry permit itself is a travel document. It contains your picture along with spaces for visas and entry and exit stamps. Re-entry permits are valid for two years and may be renewed. Persons holding Taiwanese or other passports that aren't likely to be recognised often use the re-entry permit as a travel document, instead of a passport.

If you live abroad, hold a permit to re-enter and do not file income tax returns, the INS may confiscate your green card at a port of entry. Permission to live abroad without relinquishing a permanent US residence is conditional upon filing US income tax returns.

Remember, once you have the green card, no matter where you live, keep it until the INS takes it away. There is no requirement to return the green card to the INS. The INS must prove its case before your permanent residence status is lost.

Tax returns

US tax laws require green card holders and American citizens to file tax returns and report income earned anywhere in the world. Tax treaties and credits for taxes paid to foreign governments usually eliminate double taxation. Immigrants from low-tax jurisdictions should consider the tax costs of maintaining a permanent US residence. The tax dollars, in part, pay for the services that make the US a desirable place to live. There is a price for everything!

The Internal Revenue Service (IRS) and INS exchange

information. For example, the INS reports all new green card approvals to the IRS, and both agencies maintain staff in foreign countries. The IRS will try to locate tax cheats; tax problems usually result in immigration problems. Although the lack of administrative resources prevents full-scale searches, random checks and tips from disgruntled citizens, personal enemies and jilted spouses often provide the INS and IRS with useful information.

Failure to file a tax return violates US tax laws but not immigration statutes. There is no immigration law that requires aliens to pay American taxes. However, the INS considers filing a tax return as important evidence of one's intention to maintain a permanent US residence. The tax issue may arise in various ways, outlined below.

CHEAP TAX PLANNING

Many people obtain green cards so that their children can attend school or live in the US. The parents are often quite content at home and have no intention of moving to America. Maintaining the green card requires filing a US tax return. If this increases your tax burden, and you don't want to live in the US, there's a simple solution – mail your green card back to the nearest Consulate or INS office with a letter saying you no longer wish to be a permanent resident. The children may keep their green cards because maintenance of the green card depends on the bearer, not the activities of the principal applicant. As a result your children keep their green cards and you avoid US taxes on world-wide income.

PERMITS TO RE-ENTER

The permit to re-enter form requires the applicant to promise to file US income tax returns. Failure to file may result in denial of subsequent re-entry permit applications or loss of the re-entry permit, not necessarily loss of the green card.

INS inspectors at ports of entry occasionally ask re-entry permit holders if they have filed US tax returns. If the answer is no, they may confiscate the re-entry permit. The INS inspector may also question whether the applicant has maintained a permanent US residence.

INS processing centres routinely ask re-entry permit applicants if they filed US tax returns. If the answer is negative, the INS will deny the permit application. In this case there is little risk of losing the green card as the applicant must be present in the US to apply for the re-entry permit. It is difficult for the INS to revoke a green card petition when the applicant is already in the US.

Green card
A US permanent resident who lives full-time in America but does not file US income tax returns will not lose his green card, as the US is clearly his permanent residence. This person, however, may have problems with the IRS, not the INS.

On the other hand, a US permanent resident who lives abroad for six months or more, and fails to file tax returns, may have problems with both the IRS and INS. In addition to the time spent overseas, failure to file tax returns indicates that the US is not the place of permanent residence.

When tax and immigration laws conflict
Many green card holders using tax treaty elections choose to file tax returns abroad instead of in the US. Since tax treaties supersede US domestic law, one may technically make a tax treaty election without causing a problem with the IRS or INS. Yet immigration laws view US tax returns as important evidence of permanent residence status.

What happens when the tax and immigration laws conflict? Simply put, the American judicial system has not definitively answered this question. However, common sense suggests that if the immigration benefit is more important than avoiding US tax payments, pay the tax and don't create a fight with the INS. One can argue with the

INS as a citizen without risking citizenship. But you can't argue with the INS as a permanent resident without risking loss of green card. Put another way, the IRS only wants to collect taxes – a matter of money – while the INS controls whether the individual will reside in the USA – a matter of residence. Anyone who wants to be a permanent American resident should file US income tax returns.

An example of green card forfeiture

The most common way to lose a green card is to move back to an overseas home and make only short trips to the US. This happens most often to executives, managers and business people. For example, 'Mr Smith' transfers to an overseas office while leaving his wife and children to finish school in the US. The husband commutes to visit his family. So far so good.

Mrs Smith moves to join her husband overseas, while one child stays in the US to continue schooling. The Smiths pay American income taxes but do not maintain a residence. They stay with one of their children while in the US, and their car and bills are in the child's name. Smith and his wife intend to resume living in the US once Smith retires.

During one of the Smiths' visits to their children, the INS questions them at the airport and learns the truth. The INS asks Mr Smith if he has a re-entry permit. Since Smith does not he will probably lose his green card. If Smith had a re-entry permit he wouldn't have experienced problems. He also should have taken a few other precautions. If he had planned correctly, the house, car and bills would have remained in his name. In other words, the child should have been living in Mr Smith's house, not the other way around.

The revocation of Mr Smith's green card does not mean that the child loses his green card. Although children may obtain green cards through parents, they do not lose green cards simply because the parents lost theirs. Adult children can petition for the parents at any time, and if the child is a citizen there is no quota wait. If Mr Smith has no other qualifying relatives in the US, he may take the matter to court or hope his company transfers him to the US again.

APPLYING FOR A SOCIAL SECURITY NUMBER

The **social security number (SSN)**, an identification number designed for social insurance purposes, has become the *de facto* national identification number. With few exceptions you need a social security number to open a bank account, apply for a loan, claim a tax deduction for dependants, apply for a credit card, obtain a driver's licence, receive a speeding ticket, buy a house, insurance and more.

Green card holders or persons with INS permission to work in the US may bring their INS documents to a social security office and apply on the spot. Dependants must prove their relationship to the working taxpayer. All others must provide proof of legal immigration status, identity, and a letter from the organisation requiring the social security number. This letter must specifically identify the applicant and state the reasons for requiring the SSN.

Non-residents of the US, and those without permission to work in the US, do not need an SSN. They may transact business in the US, such as opening a bank account, by filing a statement attesting to their non-resident status (Form W-8) or they may apply for a tax identification number (TIN) from the Internal Revenue Service.

SUMMARY

- Green card holders must make the US their primary and permanent residence.

- Tax laws, not immigration laws, require the filing of US tax returns.

- Filing tax returns is evidence of US permanent

residence for immigration law purposes.

- Re-entry permits allow extended absences abroad.

- Re-entry permit holders must file US tax returns as a condition for permission to remain abroad for extended periods.

- Green cards are personal. The parent's loss of a green card does not mean the children will also lose their green cards.

10

Obtaining Student Visas

Students use F-1 visas for academic programmes and M-1
visas for vocational programmes. To be eligible for either
of these visas the student must first be accepted by a
school. Once the student is accepted the school will
prepare Form I-20 for the student to submit to the INS or
to a consulate. The I-20 Form provides information about
the student's course of study and his or her means of
financial support.

The key difference between the two categories – F-1
and M-1 – is that M-1 holders may not change to H-1B
nonimmigrant status while in the US. Generally, both visa
categories are issued for the duration of the approved
educational programme. In both cases, visa procedures
may be initiated from the US or abroad.

ATTENDING PUBLIC SCHOOLS

Foreign students may only attend public (government
supported) junior high schools, and high schools for 12
months plus a 60-day grace period – and then only if the
student reimburses the public school for the cost of the
education. Local school districts, not the state or federal
government, control public education. Each school district
may set its own price. There is no restriction on attending
private schools.

Playing hooky

Students who drop out, work in violation of their student
visa or otherwise violate the terms of their student visa,
may be expelled from the US and barred from entry for
five years.

FILING FOR YOUR STUDENT VISA

The procedure for obtaining an F-1 student visa is as follows:

Step 1: Be accepted by a school.

Step 2: Obtain Form I-20 from the school. Form I-20 details the proposed course of study and estimates the financial resources necessary to complete.

Step 3: If in the US, send Form I-539 Change of Status, Form I-20 and proof of financial support to the appropriate INS regional processing centre. If the INS approves the petition, it will respond with an endorsed I-94 evidencing student status. If abroad, fill out the consular application forms, supply Form I-20 from the school as well as proof of financial support. The consul will signify approval by issuing an F-1 or M-1 visa.

TRAVELLING ON A STUDENT VISA

All students who wish to leave the US must obtain an endorsed Form I-20ID from a designated school official each time the student leaves the US. The school's endorsement proves that the student is still in school and making satisfactory progress under the approved educational programme.

Students who try to enter the US with a student visa but without an endorsed I-20ID risk denial of entry. At a minimum they must convince the INS at the port of entry of their intention to maintain an approved course of study.

Students may travel to Canada or Mexico for up to 30 days without a visa provided they have a valid I-94 and an endorsed I-20ID. All other overseas destinations require a visa. This means that the student who obtained student status in the US must ultimately return home to obtain a visa if they want to leave North America and re-enter.

PROVING FINANCIAL SUPPORT

Students must prove a source of adequate financial support. Parents, guardians or benefactors should supply an Affidavit of Support, Forms I-134 and I-864, and supply proof of sufficient funds to support the student for the duration of the approved course of study. The person signing the Affidavit of Support guarantees that the student will not use public assistance or welfare. Theoretically, this is rarely enforced; the signer of the I-134 is responsible for reimbursing the government in the event that the student uses public assistance.

STRICT ENFORCEMENT

Since many students drop out of school, work illegally or never attend classes, the INS and consuls carefully monitor F-1 or M-1 applications. Good students attending academically-respected institutions experience few difficulties, but students with average or poor grades, along with English as second-language school applicants, experience greater scrutiny. The consuls and INS want to make sure the student intends to study and not use the student visa to disappear in the US. Students must prove their credibility.

Where to get assistance

American schools often charge foreign students higher tuition fees. Indeed, some schools depend on foreign student tuition for their financial survival. Somewhere near every major American university are residences, dormitories or companies devoted to assisting the various nationalities of the college's foreign students.

Although one may always consult with an attorney, several private companies provide care and support for foreign students and will assist with visa processing. Such companies routinely care for overseas students and often help convince the consul of a student's good standing, as well as his or her intention to study while in the US.

THREE KEY QUESTIONS, THE SAME ANSWER: YES

The consuls and INS ask three key questions when reviewing student visa applications. These questions, along with the recommended answers, are listed below.

1. *Do you intend to complete a full-time course of study?* Be prepared to submit past school records and letters of recommendation from teachers as evidence.

2. *Do you have financial support?* Produce proof of adequate funds and/or show the financial statement of a sponsor on Form I-134, Affidavit of Support.

3. *Will you return to your home country after your studies are completed?* Prove this intention by demonstrating close family ties in your home country and/or a network of friends, relatives or job prospects. A course of study related to a prospective job in your home country also helps indicate your plans to return. For example, a father owns a ski lodge and resort and sends his child to the US to study hotel management. In this case, the job logically relates to the course of study.

WORKING WHILE STUDYING

The following programmes allow students to work while attending a school in the US.

On-campus employment
Any full-time student in good academic standing may work 20 hours a week at an on-campus facility during the school year and full-time between quarters or semesters.

Curricular practical training
This training must be offered in connection with a field of study. Generally, students must arrange curricular practical training with academic advisors, with the school processing the necessary paperwork. Students who work for a year or

longer in this programme lose eligibility for post-completion practical training.

POST-COMPLETION PRACTICAL TRAINING PROGRAMME

This popular programme permits students to work off-campus for one year after completion of all degree requirements. Application for this programme must be made between 90 days before and 30 days after completion of a course of study. To become eligible for this programme, first find a job and then seek the school's approval of the employment. The school files the necessary forms with the INS.

After INS approval, obtain an Employment Authorisation Card (Form I-765) to work legally. File Form I-765 and go to the nearest INS office for photographing. The Employment Authorisation Card should be available in one or two days.

Students cannot leave the US after graduation and then apply for post-completion practical training. Practical training must be approved *before* leaving the US, and students may travel after practical training approval. Students have 60 days from the end of the practical training period to depart the US, resume studies or change to another visa status.

OPTIONS AFTER PRACTICAL TRAINING

Students hoping to stay in the US after practical training have few options. They can get married to a US citizen or find a job and apply for an H-1B or an E visa. Recent university graduates usually qualify as professionals for H-1B status. Experience is not a requirement for H-1B visa professional or speciality-worker status.

Students may qualify for E visa status if they are hired by a treaty company controlled by members of their nationality. For example, a Japanese student could obtain an E visa as a professional or manager through a

Japanese-owned company.

Quite often, students and employers assume that E visas only apply to transferees from the treaty country, as when managers transfer from the home office to a US subsidiary. A treaty company may hire any qualified treaty national even if they were not previously employed by a related company abroad.

11

Visas for the Privileged, Media, Athletes, Entertainers, Cultural Exchanges, Religious Workers and Tycoons

Several lesser-used nonimmigrant visa categories deserve discussion. These include:

- I visas for persons working in information media
- O visas for outstanding artists, business people, chefs and their support staff
- P visas for professional athletes, musical groups and entertainers
- Q visas for cultural exchanges
- and R visas for religious workers.

I VISA FOR INFORMATION MEDIA

Working for the media industry

The I visa permits employees of foreign information media engaged in news-gathering or documentary material, along with key staff such as film crews and editors, to work in the US. Independent production companies qualify as long as the journalists hold credentials issued by a journalistic association. The I visa does not require university degrees or existing US trade or business. The focus is on information-gathering and reporting for news or documentary purposes, not entertainment.

An example of who is eligible for the I visa might

include a foreign television station that wished to send a journalist and editor to the US to collect material for documentary segments on American lifestyles. The journalist had over ten years' experience and a press card, but no university degree. The foreign television station agreed to support the journalist while in the US. This case was approved.

We have processed I visas for a radio show covering US lifestyle, a travelogue, a documentary discussion of Marilyn Monroe photos, as well as a Super Bowl play-by-play announcer. In all cases the applicants reported newsworthy events or created educational or documentary shows.

O VISA, A MINI GREEN CARD FOR OUTSTANDING ACTORS, BUSINESS PEOPLE AND ARTISTS

The O-category pertains to people with extraordinary skills. We often use the category as an alternative to H-1B for persons with no university degree. The O visa most commonly permits key actors and technical staff to work for motion picture, television and stage productions. Individual athletes, scientists, educators and tycoons may also qualify for O visas. We've used O visas for actors, artists, computer graphics designers in the television industry, and others. I'm proud to report that one of my O visa clients designed some of the commercials used during the 1997 Super Bowl telecast.

We have used O-1 visas to permit the producer, key technical staff and actors to come to Seattle, Washington, for the filming of the movie *The Little Buddha*. The producer, director, art people, cameramen and other key technicians had international experience and easily qualified for O-1 visa status. We filed O-2 petitions for the supporting actors and assistants.

O-visa applicants must obtain letters from an industry's professional organisation and a labour organisation attesting to their outstanding qualifications. It must be stated that there is no objection to granting a visa to the aliens. Unions often resist providing favourable letters if they believe qualified American workers exist.

The O visa may be issued for an initial validity period of three years with extensions of one year each thereafter. The O visas can be extended indefinitely, a mini green card, as long as the applicant retains his or her preeminence.

The O visa category can be used by just about anyone who is famous or internationally acclaimed in a recognised field of endeavour. Consider this category when the visa candidate does not have a university degree. Remember, the applicant must either be famous or possess esoteric skills. Otherwise, labour unions won't issue favourable advisory opinions.

WORKING AS AN ATHLETE OR ENTERTAINER

The P visa works, as a practical matter, the same as the O visa except that it applies to athletes and entertainment groups. For example, a Bunraku or Japanese puppet troupe would use P visas for the puppeteers, readers and key support staff. P visas also apply to athletic teams, boxers, sumo wrestlers and ethnic dance troupes. Validity periods depend on the length of the engagements, not to exceed five years.

Q VISA FOR CULTURAL EXCHANGE PROGRAMMES

Q visas are for cultural exchange programmes which provide a sharing of history, culture or traditions of the alien's country of nationality. The Q visa cultural exchange programme must be designed to exhibit the history, culture, religion, attitudes, philosophy or traditions of the alien's home country. The alien's employment must be connected to making the cultural exchange programme work. One of our Q visa cases was a programme hosted by an Indian restaurant that exhibited the traditions, philosophy and preparation of regional Indian cooking. The Indian restaurant used a Q visa to hire a chef to run the programme. Validity periods depend on the length of the engagements, generally not to exceed 15 months.

R VISA FOR RELIGIOUS WORKERS

At least some members of virtually every ethnic group in the world live in the US. Consider that members of any particular ethnic group divide their loyalties among several different religions. Some religions have nothing to do with ethnic affiliation, while others cater to a particular ethnic group.

For example, in Seattle, Washington, there is a Finnish Lutheran Church, a Swedish Lutheran Church and many other non-ethnic Lutheran churches. While all Lutherans, there is a special church council or governing body for the Finns and another for the Swedes. The Finns and Swedes prefer ministers who speak the native language and are trained in native customs. Many other churches, temples and synagogues have the same preference. The R visa for religious occupations satisfies this purpose.

Religious institutions catering to a particular ethnic group often make that group's members more comfortable by providing a minister or religious workers from the home country to perform services and other religious and cultural activities.

Ministers

There are no particular education requirements for an R visa. The applicant must have been a member of the church or religious organisation for at least two years prior to application. The application procedure is very simple. Apply through the INS application, or application can be made directly to the consul by letter. The visa is usually valid for three years with a two-year extension. The R visa is very flexible and available to all religions. There is also a green card category available to religious workers. The requirements are very similar to the R visa, and religious workers are exempt from labour certification.

I never gave this category much thought until a few

years ago when we helped Buddhist nuns from Taiwan. I assumed that any woman who shaved her head, wore a nondescript saffron robe, and bore ritual tattoos and burn marks could be considered a legitimate Buddhist. I was wrong. The INS gently informed me that Taiwanese and Thai businessmen and women, in particular, often give large donations to a temple, disguise themselves as monks or nuns, and apply for an R visa and then a green card as a religious worker. Very clever. This is an abused category, so be prepared to carefully document your religious convictions and affiliation. The more strict consuls require ritual by fire.

When a pastor of the Finnish Lutheran Church in Seattle passed away the church members wanted a Finnish replacement. The new replacement was ordained by the governing body of the church, studied religion at the university level, and had over two years' experience. The church is a nonprofit religious organisation. This case more than met the legal requirements for an R visa. Although ministers do not have to graduate from a university, they must be ordained or be able to prove they have authority to conduct religious worship. Religious workers also need two years' experience with a particular religious organisation immediately prior to transfer to the US.

Religious workers

Another case arose when a religious outreach programme, again Lutheran, needed a social worker to direct an outreach programme to help refugees from Somalia, Eritrea and Ethiopia. The refugees were having trouble adjusting to life in the US, and the church-sponsored outreach programme provided social and religious counselling services as well as religious training. The programme did not require a minister but needed a social worker with Lutheran training.

The applicant had a nursing degree plus two years of religious training and over two years' experience providing religious comfort to sick people in Lutheran hospitals in Finland. The applicant had worked for a Lutheran hospital for over two years. This applicant's credentials exceeded the minimum requirements.

R visa religious workers may include counsellors, social workers, health-care workers for religious hospitals, missionaries, translators, religious broadcasters and just about any other occupation necessary to a religious organisation. The term 'religious worker' does not include janitors, fund raisers and people removed from the religion. An exception to this is seen in the few religions where the janitor must follow religious practices.

DETAILS ABOUT NAFTA

The North American Free Trade Agreement (NAFTA) provides additional nonimmigrant visa categories mostly for professional workers (designated TN) for citizens of Mexico and Canada to work in the US. The reverse applies for US citizens wishing to work in Mexico or Canada. The complete list of NAFTA categories is available from the US, Canadian or Mexico consulates. The list is also available in the Federal Register, Site 8C.F.R., Section 214.6 (c).

Additionally under NAFTA, Canadians may apply for L-1 or H-1 status at specified land border crossings or airports. Mexicans must continue to apply through INS regional processing centres. For Canadians the NAFTA filing procedures avoid processing delays incurred at INS regional processing centres.

Expedited procedures for Canadians under NAFTA
Canadian TN applicants may apply at land border ports of entry and designated airports. Applications simply consist of a cover letter explaining eligibility for the particular category and documented proof, such as university transcripts or verification of required experience. No additional forms are necessary. Border processing usually occurs on the spot, and generally takes no longer than a couple of days. The INS evidences Treaty National status

by issuing an I-94 card endorsed 'TN'.

All Treaty Nationals may work in the US for periods of up to one year, and TN status may be renewed annually. Although NAFTA does not limit the number of extensions available to TN visa holders, common sense dictates that the INS will question frequent extension applicants.

Strategy

The NAFTA visas afford Canadians fast processing with minimal paperwork when the system works. Processing procedures and policies vary among the border-crossing posts. Some posts process petitions on the spot while others prefer to review copies before interviewing the applicant. Enforcement policies also vary; some posts are stricter than others. Since the situation constantly changes, we advise NAFTA applicants to check for local procedures before applying at a border post.

Most NAFTA applicants also qualify for H, L or E visa status. NAFTA works for those who wish to work in the US for a short period of time, or for those who need to quickly start work in America. Once in the US, NAFTA applicants may change to a longer-term nonimmigrant visa, such as H-1, E-1/2 or L-1A.

It is important to note that all NAFTA visas automatically expire upon application for labour certification or permanent residence. Because NAFTA visas only last one year and permanent residence processing takes more than one year, it is important to change from a NAFTA status to another non-immigrant status that lasts more than one year, such as E, H, or L, before applying for permanent residence status. Otherwise, the NAFTA visa holder will find themselves out of status in the US, out of job in the US and must return to Canada to wait for the permanent residence visa to be approved.

SELF ASSESSMENT

Nonimmigrant visas

- You are taking a trip for business or pleasure: use visa waiver. If the trip exceeds 90 days or you do not qualify for visa waiver: use B1/2.

- You have a university degree: you may qualify for H-1B if you can find a job.

- You have unique skills or outstanding accomplishments: use O1; and if you have a university degree O1 or H-1B.

- You work for a multinational company in a managerial position: L1A or E1/2. If you also have a university degree: H-1B.

- You own your own company and want to set up a US operation: as above.

- You don't own your own company and you want to make a US investment: consider E2.

- You don't own your own company and you want to import or export goods or services from the US: consider E1.

- None of the above applies, but no US worker meets the minimum job requirements: H2.

Green cards

- You marry a US citizen or have US parents: immediate relative.

- You have US permanent resident spouse or parents: 2nd preference but be prepared to wait at least two years.

- You have US citizen brothers or sisters: 4th preference but be prepared to wait.

- You work for a multinational corporation as a manager or higher: multi-national manager, one of the simplest ways to get a green card.

- You have extraordinary skills: pass Go, collect $200.

- You have exceptional skills in US national interests: national interest waiver.

- You are an outstanding researcher at academic or research institution: let your employer take care of the visa processing.

- None of the above: you must go through labour certification or invest at least $500,000.

12

Naturalisation: Becoming an American Citizen

Most countries of the world base citizenship on parentage, and try to limit citizenship to particular ethnic heritage. For example, a person born in Japan or France must have a Japanese or French parent to become a citizen. Many countries require a male qualifying parent, while a few nations require a female qualifying parent. Recently, many countries have eliminated the sex discrimination but retained the parentage requirement.

America, a country open to all ethnic groups, automatically grants citizenship to any person born in the US, regardless of parental nationality and why or how long the parents were in the country. Persons born in America merely need to present a birth certificate to apply for a passport. Otherwise, US citizenship, with few exceptions, requires the passage of time as a green card resident, basic knowledge of US history and government, and an ability to speak English.

Because many people plan to give birth to a child in the US (for automatic citizenship), there is some talk about requiring a greater than nine-month residency requirement. This is known in the trade as 'baby droppers'.

People over 55 who have resided in the US for 20 years or more do not have to meet the language requirement. After all, how does someone live in the US for 20 years and avoid learning English? Amazingly, such people do exist.

ADVANTAGES OF CITIZENSHIP

There are two practical advantages of US citizenship: You can vote, and it's hard to lose citizen status. You can lose citizenship if you lied to get a green card, failed to disclose past crimes, or perjured a material fact relating to citizenship or a green card. Unlike aliens who can lose their green card as a result of prolonged absence from the US, American citizens may leave the country and return at any time without fear of losing citizenship.

Every American citizen can vote. Since permanent residents are taxpayers, they want to have a say about the amount of income tax and how it's spent. There are many other important reasons to vote.

DUAL CITIZENSHIP

The US permits dual nationality. American citizens of dual nationality must consult the other country about holding two passports. The US government does not inquire or even care if a person owns two passports. For example, a US citizen holding US and Japanese passports may risk losing his Japanese passport to the Japanese government, but not the US passport.

THE QUALIFYING PERIOD

A green card spouse of a US citizen must reside in the US for three years before becoming eligible for citizenship. All other permanent residents must reside in the US for five years. If your American spouse dies while you have a green card, you still may qualify under the three-year rule.

You must live in the US for six months or more in each consecutive year. With few exceptions, a break in residence restarts the qualifying period at the beginning. If you work abroad without obtaining a re-entry permit and return seven months later, you will lose the year for citizenship-qualifying purposes, and must begin the qualification period again.

A hypothetical example of this is seen when a green card graduate student goes abroad for a year of field work without obtaining a re-entry permit. While abroad the student remains registered with an American university. The one year abroad breaks the citizenship qualification period, and the student must wait five more years before applying for citizenship. Obtaining a re-entry permit would have prevented restarting the qualifying period, but time abroad would not have counted.

THE CITIZENSHIP TEST

Upon meeting the residency requirements, you may file for naturalisation at any INS District Office. File the appropriate form (N-400), which includes biographical information and proof of required residence. The INS will schedule an interview for the person to be tested on US history and government. Only those who meet the 55–20 requirement (be 55 years or older and have 20 years at residency in the US) will avoid being tested in English. English language ability is a citizenship requirement.

The test questions are the same sorts of things most Americans learn in junior high schools. Several books are available in libraries and book stores to provide sample questions and study aids. Most immigration examiners ask reasonable questions. Examiners tend to ask difficult questions when they suspect the applicant did not study. Sample questions could include:

'Do you know how many congressmen comprise the Senate and House of Representatives?'

'Can you name the first five Presidents in order?'

'Do you know who was the President of the Confederacy?'

INS examiners tend to be understanding of those who studied for the test. When asked, 'Who was George

Washington?' one of my clients answered, 'My first son.'
Confused, the elderly woman, with help from the INS
examiner, managed to regain her composure and pass the
test. In another case a young Chinese woman, laden with
gold jewellery and who obviously didn't study, was
rejected after she failed to identify the metal responsible
for the California Gold Rush. (By the way, the Chinese
characters for San Francisco translate to 'Gold
Mountain'.) This woman had made no attempt to learn
English and the examiner was looking for a way for her
to fail the test.

OBTAINING A CERTIFICATE OF NATURALISATION

Upon passing the citizenship test and residency
requirements, a citizenship paper (called the 'Certificate of
Naturalisation') can be obtained from the INS or a federal
court. Name changes are permissible at the time of
naturalisation, if so desired.

The INS procedure is faster and the federal court
procedure, scheduled every few months, is more elaborate.
In the court procedure the judge says a few kind words,
the citizenship candidates pledge allegiance to the US, and
they then receive naturalisation certificates.

Many people prefer the more elaborate federal court
ceremony to commemorate this important event. On the
4th of July, Independence Day in the US, most American
cities hold a large citizenship ceremony. People from all
over the world, with different backgrounds, experience
and personal stories of how they came to the US, become
American citizens at the same time. We call this American
phenomenon the 'melting pot', whereby people from all
over the world become citizens of the United States of
America.

PRACTICAL POINTERS FOR NATURALISATION APPLICANTS

- You can file six months before you are technically eligible.

- You must live in the INS district where you file for the six-month period prior to filing.

- Expect the process to take a year, often more.

- Lawyers can't make the process faster.

- We stopped taking routine naturalisation cases unless there are special circumstances. In most US cities you will find naturalisation classes that take the applicant through the test and filing procedure.

- INS often tries to use naturalisation as a lever to entice tax cheats to pay up. This practice is actually against the law. As a practical matter, it's better to pay up than experience significant delays in processing while you argue about your rights.

- There are expedited procedures for military personnel.

13

Thoughts for Human Resource Managers and Employees

Overseas relocation requires consideration of the needs of the family, not just the employee. Changes in life style, education, environment and career can disrupt seemingly stable families. Employees often feel they must choose between the commitment to their careers and to their families.

The employee's willingness to relocate, and their future job performance, can be affected by damaged family relationships caused by a spouse having to give up a career, unsettled children who cannot cope at schools, the elderly relatives left behind. Why take a risk on moving? It's not just a matter of career and remuneration.

Many employees and their families find overseas relocation frustrating and difficult. The amount of information and advice required for a smooth transition can be overwhelming. Inaccurate advice may result in ill will towards the employer.

The HR professional must not only sell the concept of moving for positive reasons, but also ensure a smooth landing for the entire family. Despite the risks and expenses, overseas assignments will dramatically increase in years to come as the rate of business globalisation increases.

WHY SEND AN EMPLOYEE OVERSEAS?

The expatriate may:

- Act as a representative of the parent company, responsible for the whole business, which demands an extensive range of management skills that would not be learned at home.

- Be responsible for maintaining the corporate culture and control over newly created or acquired subsidiaries.

- Alleviate a shortage of specialised skills not available locally.

- Act as a liaison between the head office and the foreign subsidiary.

- Enable the company to maintain its identity and serve their own nationals. For example, the Japanese airline needs to employ mostly Japanese crews so that they can communicate and serve their Japanese customers better.

UNDERSTANDING WHY EMPLOYEES WANT TO GO ABROAD

The successful HR manager creates excitement around the opportunity to live and work abroad. They promote the 'good' reasons to move rather than threaten the employee with retribution if he refuses to relocate.

Many employees see relocation as a personal challenge, some view it as a professional opportunity, some take the chance because of a higher salary and some may want to experience other cultures. There are also those who are fed up with the management style at home or see this opportunity as a fresh start or the only way of progressing. Some view it as a chance to send their children to top schools at company expense. The expatriate can enjoy the best of the host country without worrying about living there forever.

EASING THE TRANSITION TO OVERSEAS LIFE

Manning a foreign post can be a lonely and stressful task for some, an opportunity for others. The reaction of family members may influence the relocated employee's job performance. The transition to overseas life works smoothly when the family unit makes a happy landing abroad.

Information and support are key to easing the transition to overseas life. Avoid conflict that can interfere with employees' productivity and corporate objectives by listening and responding to employees' needs, however mundane, at the beginning of the transfer. Encourage employees and their families to maintain a sense of control over the process by:

1   Providing adequate information.
2   Providing approachable communication.
3   Taking a flexible approach to service provision.

Explaining important differences

The US state and Federal governments, compared with most industrial countries, provide a minimum of social services. Many relocated employees are surprised by how much they must do for themselves. Although this system tends to keep taxes lower, the uninitiated must be prepared.

Remember, the USA does not provide national health insurance. The countless variations among company health plans, preferred provider organisations, health maintenance organisations, co-operative health organisations, fee for service health plans, all require explanation.

Drunk driving laws require attention. Most US cities do not have adequate public transport. This means you must drive home from the pub or party. In most states the alcohol limit is .08, or two beers. The penalty is usually suspension of the driver's licence, plus a fine. As a result car insurance, all privately provided, will become prohibitively expensive or nonexistent.

It is useful to provide a list of favourite food stores, restaurants and pubs, a referral to a local lawyer and accountant, tips on local idiosyncrasies, and driver licence information. The employee is starting again, the HR professional must assist in the process or the employee will spend too much time getting adjusted rather than working.

Working spouses

The needs of spouses have become a major issue. Relocation packages should account for the needs of dual career couples. Relocation can put an immense strain on a relationship; it may ruin the marriage. Many international assignments do not succeed because the non-employee spouse cannot work in the foreign country even if they can find a job. It's difficult for the non-working spouse to separate from friends, family and sometimes a career to stay home and do nothing in a foreign country.

Employers should provide career help for the non-working spouse. Individuals should consider this issue before they embark on their US adventure. The spouse of a green card holder can work without restriction. The spouse of a nonimmigrant employee cannot work without a visa permitting employment. There is usually a way to accommodate the non-employee spouse with a university degree. Simply put, no university degree, no visa, no job.

RELOCATION TIPS FOR COMPANY EMPLOYEES AND INDIVIDUALS

Ask lots of questions. For example:

- How flexible is the relocation package?
- What provisions are there for keeping the family together during the relocation?
- Who will talk to my partner?
- What happens if I can't sell my house?
- How much time do I have to look for a new place?
- To what extent can I control the timing of the move?
- Can you arrange a working visa for my spouse?
- Where will my children go to school, and who pays?
- What personal belongings may I bring without customs duty?

- Can I ship my car or should I buy a new one?

- Who will provide health insurance?

- What company relocation allowances are available?

- Who pays moving and travel costs?

- Who takes the risks of currency fluctuations?

- Will an acceptable position be waiting when I return?

- Will time abroad count towards company retirement benefits?

Preparing for everyday differences

Then there are all the mundane questions ranging from the local electrical current, to the location of the dry cleaners.

Some easy answers to the above. You can bring household effects to the USA duty free. Don't ship the car because foreign cars must be fitted with expensive, performance reducing pollution control devices. Most foreign household appliances, particularly CD players, don't work well on US current even with an adaptor.

Try to learn about US cultural differences before leaving home. The US is a big country. There are regional cultural differences. There is an American-UK or other country chamber of commerce chapter in most US and foreign major cities. These organisations often provide social contacts and help with the particulars of living in the USA.

Planning your return

Whether you come to the US as an individual investor or employee, plan an exit strategy. Repatriation can be as hard as adjusting to overseas life. The world did not stop just because you moved overseas. Be prepared to make new friends, get used to the new work environment and, probably, a new boss and position.

International relocation becomes more common every day. Since the costs of relocating in both human and financial terms are very high, preparation is necessary to get the process right.

Appendix 1
Immigration Forms and Other Documents

FORMS REQUIRING NO FILING FEES

The following forms require no filing fees. Forms are available from the US Government Printing Office or a local INS office.

Form number	Title
ETA 750 part A & B	Application for Labor Certification
ETA-9035	Labor condition application (part of H-1B filing)
G-325	Biographical (usually used in the US only)
I-9	Confirmation of Authority to Work
OF-156	Visa Application/Revalidation
OF-179	Document Checklist (Embassy)
OF-230 part 1 & 2	Biographical (Embassy)
I-245	Affidavit at Support (for employment-based applicants)
I-864	Affidavit of Support (for family-class applicants)

FORMS REQUIRING FEES

Since filing fees change frequently, we won't include them in book. For an updated Fee List contact an INS centre.

Form number	Title
I-17	Petition for Approval of School for Attendance by Nonimmigrant Students
I-90	Application to Replace Alien Registration Card

I-102	Application for Replacement/Initial Nonimmigrant Arrival-Departure Document
I-129	Petition for Nonimmigrant Worker
I-129E	Supplement for E Visa
I-129F	Petition for Alien Fiancé(e)
I-129H	Supplement for H Visas
I-129L	Supplement for L Visas
I-130	Petition for Alien Relative
I-131	Application for Travel Document/Request for Advance Parole
I-140	Petition for Prospective Immigrant Employee
I-191	Application for Advance Permission to Return to Unrelinquished Domicile
I-192	Application for Advanced Permission to Enter as Nonimmigrant
I-193	Application for Waiver of Passport and/or Visa
I-212	Application for Permission to Reapply for Admission into the United States After Deportation or Removal
I-246	Application for Stay of Deportation
I-256A	Application for Suspension of Deportation
I-290A	Notice of Appeal to the Board of Immigration Appeals
I-290B	Notice of Appeal to the Administrative Appeal Unit
I-360	Petition for Amerasian, Widow(er), or Special Immigrant (except there is no fee for a petition seeking classification as an Amerasian)
I-485	Application for Permanent Residence
I-526	Immigrant Petition by Alien Entrepreneur
I-539	Application to Extend/Change Nonimmigrant Status
I-600	Petition to Classify Orphan as an Immediate Relative
I-600A	Application for Advance Processing of Orphan Petition
I-601	Application for Waiver of Grounds of

154 Getting into America

	Excludability
I-612	Application for Waiver of the Foreign Residence Requirement
I-690	Application for Waiver of Grounds of Excludability (replaced by I-601)
I-694	Notice of Appeal of Decision under Section 210 or 245A of the Immigration and Nationality Act
I-695	Application for Replacement of Form I-688A, Employment Authorization for Form I-688, Temporary Residence Card
I-698	Application to Adjust Status from Temporary to Permanent Resident
I-751	Petition to Remove the Conditions of Residence
I-765	Application for Employment Authorization
I-817	Application for Voluntary Departure Under the Family Unity Program
I-821	Application for Temporary Protected Status
I-823	Application for Participation in a Dedicated Commuter Lane Program
I-824	Application for Action on an Approval Application or Petition
I-907	Request for Premium Processing
Motions	Motions to Reopen or Reconsider
N-300	Application to File Declaration of Intention
N-336	Request for Hearing on a Decision Naturalisation Processing
N-400	Application for Naturalisation
N-410	Motion for Amendment of Petition (Application)
N-455	Application for Transfer of Petition for Naturalisation
N-470	Application to Preserve Residence for Naturalisation Purposes
N-565	Application for Replacement Naturalisation Purposes
N-600	Application for Certificate of Citizenship
N-643	Application for Certificate of Citizenship on Behalf of an Adopted Child
N-644	Application for Posthumous Citizenship

Appendix 2
Visa Categories

NONIMMIGRANT VISA CATEGORIES

Here is a list of virtually all of the nonimmigrant visa categories. Some of the lesser used categories have been combined into one description. All visa categories are designated by letters of the alphabet. Subcategories are designated by numbers. For example, L is the letter designating visas for international organisations. L-1 is for the principal applicant, L-2 is for dependants. 'Dependants' means spouse and children under 21 years of age.

A-1 to A-3 Diplomats, public ministers, dependants and personal attendants.

B-1 Business visitors.

B-2 Tourist visitors.

C-1 Travellers in transit through the US.

D-1 Airline or ship crew.

E-1 Treaty trader.

E-2 Treaty investor

F-1 Academic and language training students.

G-1 to G-5 Representatives of foreign governments and employers of quasi-governmental international organisations and some United Nations employees, servants and dependants.

NATO-1 to
NATO-5 Certain employees and military personnel of the North Atlantic Treaty Organisation, dependants and servants.

H-1A Registered nurses.

H-1B	Speciality occupations and professionals.
H-2A	Temporary or seasonal agricultural workers unavailable in the US.
H-2B	Other temporary or seasonal workers unavailable in the US.
H-3	Temporary trainees learning skills unavailable in their home country.
H-4	Immediate family of H visa classifications.
I	Foreign press and information media coming to report on newsworthy or informational events as opposed to selling entertainment.
J-1	Exchange visitors coming as part of a United States Information Agency-approved exchange programme.
J-2	Dependants of J visa holders.
K-1	Fiancé(e)s of US citizens who intend to marry within 90 days of entry.
L-1	Intracompany transferees in an executive, managerial or specialised knowledge capacity.
L-2	L-1 dependants.
M-1	Vocational school students.
M-2	M-1 dependants.
O-1	Individuals of extraordinary ability in the arts, sciences, business, professions or athletics
O-2	Essential support staff of O-1 aliens.
O-3	O visa dependants.
P-1	Internationally-renowned artists, athletes and entertainers and their support staff.
P-2	Entertainers coming to perform at a government approved cultural exchange programme.
P-3	Culturally-unique entertainers.
P-4	P visa dependants.
Q-1	Participants in international cultural exchange programmes; may be privately sponsored.
Q-2	Q visa dependants.
R-1	Ministers and religious workers.
R-2	R visa dependants.
S	International terrorist informants.

V   Spouse of US permanent residences who have
           already waited three years for their priority
           date can come to the US to join their US
           spouse.

TN   North American Free Trade Agreement
           (NAFTA) nationals.

PERMANENT RESIDENT VISA CATEGORIES
Family Sponsored Preferences
First Preference: Unmarried sons and daughters of citizens.
Second Preference: Spouses and children, and unmarried
sons and daughters of permanent residents.
Third Preference: Married sons and daughters of citizens.
Fourth Preferences: Brothers and sisters of adult citizens.

Employment-Based Preferences
First Preference: Priority workers, international managers.
Second Preference: Members of professions holding
advanced degrees or persons of exceptional ability.
Third Preference: Skilled workers, professionals and other
workers.
Fourth Preference: Certain special immigrants.
Fifth Preference: Employment creation.

Appendix 3
Important Addresses

IMMIGRATION & NATURALIZATION SERVICE CENTERS

Eastern

The Eastern INS Service Center has jurisdiction over the following states: Massachusetts, Connecticut, New Hampshire, Rhode Island, New York, Pennsylvania, Delaware, Washington D.C., West Virginia, Maryland, New Jersey, Virginia, Maine and Vermont.

It also has jurisdiction over the following INS offices: Puerto Rico, Bermuda, Toronto, Montreal, Virgin Islands and Dominican Republic.

> Eastern INS Service Centre
> 75 Lower Welden Street
> St Albans, VT 05479-0001
> Tel: (802) 527-3160

Northern

The Northern INS Service Centre has jurisdiction over the following states: Michigan, Illinois, Indiana, Wisconsin, Oregon, Alaska, Minnesota, North Dakota, South Dakota, Kansas, Missouri, Washington, Idaho, Colorado, Utah, Wyoming, Ohio, Nebraska and Iowa.

It also has jurisdiction over the following INS offices: Manitoba, British Columbia and Calgary.

> Northern INS Service Centre
> Federal Building and US Courthouse
> 850 'S' Street
> Lincoln, NE 68501
> Tel: (402) 437-5218 or (402) 437-5464

Southern

The Southern INS Service Center has jurisdiction over the following states: Florida, Texas, New Mexico, Oklahoma, Georgia, North Carolina, South Carolina, Alabama, Louisiana, Arkansas, Mississippi, Tennessee and Kentucky.

It also has jurisdiction over the following INS offices: Bahamas, Freeport and Nassau.

Southern INS Service Centre
PO Box 15122
Department 'A'
Irving, TX 75015-2122
Tel: (214) 767-7769

Western

The Western INS Service Center has jurisdiction over the following states and territory: California, Hawaii, Arizona, Nevada and Guam.

For expedite and courier deliveries:

Western INS Service Center
24000 Avila Road
2nd Floor, Room 2304
Laguna Niguel, CA 92677
Attn: Incoming Mailroom

For regular mail:
PO Box 30111
Laguna Niguel, CA 92677-8011

CONSULATES

Each foreign country has its own consular office. Look in your local telephone directory for the consulate nearest you.

VISA OFFICE

US Visa Office
2401 East Street N.W.
Washington, D.C. 20520

Appendix 4
Suggested Document Lists

Here are the suggested document lists for the various visa applications. The documents listed are necessary for background information for a particular visa petition.

E-1 TREATY TRADER VISA APPLICATION

1. Information concerning parent company
a. Articles of Incorporation, seal page only
b. Financial Statement
c. Company brochure and general description of business
d. Organisational chart, number of employees and general job titles
e. Business goal in the US
f. Shareholders, percent ownership and nationality
g. In case of holding companies, supply description of business activities of principal investors or shareholders.

2. Information concerning the US company or enterprise
a. Articles of Incorporation and organisational documents
b. Financial Statement and Pro Forma for start-up
c. Description of business goals in the US
d. US organisational chart and staffing requirements
e. Evidence of initial and continuing investment: *ie*, currency transfers and invoices
f. Job description of transferee
g. Amount and proof of trade between the US and

foreign company; *ie*, invoices, shipping document samples, in-house accounting, computer, *etc*.
h. Proof of US investment, trade activities, currency transfers, *etc*.

3. Information concerning the alien

a. Personal data, name, date of birth, address in foreign country in last two years
b. Resumé detailing complete employment history with salaries for recent jobs
c. Educational history
d. Biographical details regarding accompanying family members, if any.

E-2 TREATY INVESTOR VISA APPLICATION

1. Information concerning parent company

a. Articles of Incorporation, seal page only
b. Financial Statement
c. Company brochure and general description of business
d. Organisational chart, number of employees and general job
   titles
e. Corporate ownership of parent company; documents substantiating each tier of ownership, *ie*, trusts or holding companies. Stock registers and the first page of the organisational documents of each entity generally suffice. Copies of passports for each shareholder.

2. Information concerning the US company or enterprise

a. Articles of Incorporation, first page only
b. Financial Statement
c. Description of business, business plan, Pro Forma financial statement
d. US organisational chart
e. Lease or proof of ownership of US premises

f. Job descriptions
g. Amount of capital invested in US business; documents evidencing transfer of funds from parent company to US subsidiary and application of funds
h. Proof of ownership of US company, *ie* stock register.

3. Information concerning the alien

a. Personal data, name, date and place of birth, address in foreign company
b. Resumé detailing employment history and salaries
c. Educational history
d. Details regarding accompanying family members, if any.

H-1 PROFESSIONAL VISA APPLICATION

1. Information concerning the employee

a. University degree(s)
b. Complete resumé with date and place of birth, home address abroad, address in the US, list of prior employers with your job description at each place of employment.
c. Your salary with US employer

2. Information about the US employer

a. Articles of Incorporation for the US employer
b. Gross and net annual income of the US employer; if company is a start-up, send a Pro Forma financial statement
c. Brochure, if any, for US employer or its corporate group.

L-1 (INTRACOMPANY TRANSFEREES IN AN EXECUTIVE, MANAGERIAL OR SPECIALIZED KNOWLEDGE CAPACITY) VISA APPLICATION

I. Information concerning the parent company

a. Articles of Incorporation

b. Financial Statement
c. Company brochure and general description of business
d. Organisational chart, number of employees and general job
    titles
c. Corporate ownership of parent company; documents substantiating each tier of ownership, *ie*, trusts or holding companies. Stock registers and the first page of the organisational documents of each entity generally suffice. Copies of passports for each shareholder.

2. Information concerning the US company or enterprise

a. Articles of Incorporation and organisational documents
b. Pro Forma financial statement
c. Description of business
d. Proposed US organisational chart
e. Lease or proof of ownership of US premises
f. Applicant's job description
g. Amount of capital invested in US business; documents evidencing transfer of funds from parent company to US subsidiary
h. Proof of ownership of US company, *ie*, stock register
i. Federal tax identification number.

3. Information concerning the alien

a. Personal data; name, date and place of birth, address in foreign company
b. Resumé detailing employment history and salaries for most recent position and last residence addresses
c. Educational history
d. Details regarding accompanying family members, if any.

Appendix 5
Typical Citizenship Questions

DEPARTMENT OF JUSTICE, IMMIGRATION AND NATURALZATION SERVICE: 100 TYPICAL QUESTIONS

1. What are the colours of our flag?
2. How many stars are there in our flag?
3. What colour are the stars on our flag?
4. What do the stars on the flag mean?
5. How many stripes are there in the flag?
6. What colour are the stripes?
7. What do the stripes on the flag mean?
8. How many states are there in the Union?
9. What is the 4th of July?
10. What is the date of Independence Day?
11. Independence from whom?
12. What country did we fight during the Revolutionary War?
13. Who was the first President of the United States?
14. Who is the President of the United States today?
15. Who is the Vice-President of the United States today?
16. Who elects the President of the United States?
17. Who becomes President of the United States if the President should die?
18. For how long do we elect the President?
19. What is the Constitution?
20. Can the Constitution be changed?
21. What do we call changes to the Constitution?
22. How many changes or amendments are there to the Constitution?
23. How many branches are there in our government?
24. What are the three branches of our government?
25. What is the Legislative branch of our government?
26. Who makes the laws in the United States?

27. What is Congress?
28. What are the duties of Congress?
29. Who elects Congress?
30. How many senators are there in Congress?
31. Can you name the two senators from your State?
32. For how long do we elect each senator?
33. How many representatives are there in Congress?
34. For how long do we elect the representatives?
35. What is the Executive branch of our government?
36. What is the Judiciary branch of our government?
37. What are the duties of the Supreme Court?
38. What is the supreme law of the United States?
39. What is the Bill of Rights?
40. What is the capital of your State?
41. Who is the current governor of your State?
42. Who becomes President of the US if the President and the Vice-President should die?
43. Who is the Chief Justice of the Supreme Court?
44. Can you name the 13 original states?
45. Who said, 'Give me liberty or give me death'?
46. Which countries were our enemies during World War II?
47. What are the 49th and 50th states of the union?
48. How many terms can a President serve?
49. Who was Martin Luther King, Jr.?
50. Who is the head of your local government?
51. According to the Constitution, a person must meet certain requirements in order to be eligible to become President. Name one of these requirements.
52. Why are there 100 senators in the Senate?
53. Who selects the Supreme Court Justices?
54. How many Supreme Court Justices are there?
55. Why did the Pilgrims come to America?
56. What is the head executive of a state government called?
57. What is the head executive of a city government called?
58. What holiday was celebrated for the first time by the American Colonists?
59. Who was the main writer of the Declaration of Independence?
60. When was the Declaration of Independence adopted?
61. What is the basic belief of the Declaration of Independence?
62. What is the National Anthem of the United States?

63. Who wrote the Star-Spangled Banner?
64. Where does freedom of speech come from?
65. What is the minimum voting age in the United States?
66. Who signs Bills into law?
67. What is the highest court in the United States?
68. Who was the President during the Civil War?
69. What did the Emancipation Proclamation do?
70. What special group advises the President?
71. Which President is called the 'Father of our Country'?
72. What Immigration and Naturalization Service form is used to apply to become a naturalized citizen?
73. Who helped the Pilgrims in America?
74. What is the name of the ship that brought the Pilgrims to America?
75. What were the 13 original States of the United States called?
76. Name three rights or freedoms guaranteed by the Bill of Rights.
77. Who has the Power to Declare War?
78. What kind of government does the United States have?
79. Which President freed the slaves?
80. In what year was the Constitution written?
81. What are the first ten amendments to the Constitution called?
82. Name one purpose of the United Nations.
83. Where does Congress meet?
84. Whose rights are guaranteed by the Constitution and the Bill of Rights?
85. What is the introduction to the Constitution called?
86. Name one benefit of being a citizen of the United States.
87. What is the most important right granted to US citizens?
88. What is the United States Capitol?
89. What is the White House?
90. Where is the White House located?
91. What is the name of the President's official home?
92. Name one right guaranteed by the first amendment?
93. Who is the Commander in Chief of the US Military?
94. Which President was the first Commander in Chief of the US Military?
95. In what month do we vote for the President?
96. In what month is the new President inaugurated?
97. How many times may a senator be re-elected?

98. How many times may a congressman be re-elected?
99. What are the two major political parties in the US today?
100. How many States are there in the United States?

ANSWERS

1.   Red, white and blue
2.   50
3.   White
4.   One for each State in the Union
5.   13
6.   Red and white
7.   They represent the original 13 States
8.   50
9.   Independence Day
10. 4th July
11. England
12. England
13. George Washington
14. Bill Clinton
15. Al Gore
16. The electoral college
17. Vice President
18. Four years
19. The Supreme Law of the Land
20. Yes
21. Amendments
22. 26
23. 3
24. Legislative, Executive and Judiciary
25. Congress
26. Congress
27. The Senate and the House of Representatives
28. To make laws
29. The people
30. 100
31. (Insert local information)
32. 6 years
33. 435
34. 2 years
35. The President, Cabinet, and departments under the cabinet members

36. The Supreme Court
37. To interpret laws
38. The Constitution
39. The first 10 amendments of the Constitution
40. (Insert local information)
41. (Insert local information)
42. Speaker of the House of Representatives
43. William Rehnquist
44. Connecticut, New Hampshire, New York, New Jersey, Massachusetts, Pennsylvania, Delaware, Virginia, North Carolina, South Carolina, Georgia, Rhode Island and Maryland
45. Patrick Henry
46. Germany, Italy and Japan
47. Hawaii and Alaska
48. 2
49. A civil rights leader
50. (Insert local information)
51. Must be a natural born citizen of the United States; must be at least 35 years old by the time he/she will serve; must have lived in the United States for at least 14 years
52. 2 from each State
53. Appointed by the President
54. 9
55. For religious freedom
56. Governor
57. Mayor
58. Thanksgiving
59. Thomas Jefferson
60. 4th July 1776
61. That all men are created equal
62. The Star-Spangled Banner
63. Francis Scott Key
64. The Bill of Rights
65. 18
66. The President
67. The Supreme Court
68. Abraham Lincoln
69. Freed the slaves
70. The Cabinet
71. George Washington
72. Form N-400, 'Application to file petition for

naturalization'

73. The American Indians (Native Americans)
74. *The Mayflower*
75. Colonies
76. A. The right of freedom of speech, press, religion, peaceable assembly and requesting change of government.
    B. The right to bear arms (the right to have weapons or own a gun, though subject to certain regulations).
    C. The government may not quarter, or house, soldiers in people's homes during peacetime without the people's consent.
    D. The government may not search or take a person's property without a warrant.
    E. A person may not be tried twice for the same crime and does not have to testify against him/herself.
    F. A person charged with a crime still has some rights, such as the right to a trial and to have a lawyer.
    G. The right to trial by jury in most cases.
    H. Protects people against excessive or unreasonable fines or cruel and unusual punishment.
    I. The people have rights other than those mentioned in the Constitution.
    J. Any power not given to the federal government by the Constitution is a power of either the State or the people.

77. The Congress
78. Republican
79. Abraham Lincoln
80. 1787
81. The Bill of Rights
82. For countries to discuss and try to resolve world problems, to provide economic aid to many countries.
83. In the Capitol in Washington, D.C.
84. Everyone's (citizens and non-citizens living in the US)
85. The Preamble
86. Obtain federal government jobs, travel with a US passport, petition for close relatives to come to the US to live
87. The right to vote
88. The place where Congress meets

89. The President's official home
90. Washington D.C. (1600 Pennsylvania Avenue N.W.)
91. The White House
92. Freedom of speech, press, religion, peaceable assembly and requesting change of the government
93. The President
94. George Washington
95. November
96. January
97. There is no limit
98. There is no limit
99. Democratic and Republican
100. 50

Appendix 6
Some Sample Forms

NOTICE OF ENTRY OF APPEARANCE AS ATTORNEY OR REPRESENTATIVE

In re:	DATE
	FILE No.

I hereby enter my appearance as attorney for (or representative of), and at the request of, the following named person(s):

NAME	☐ Petitioner ☐ Beneficiary	☐ Applicant
ADDRESS (Apt. No.) (Number & Street) (City)	(State)	(ZIP Code)

NAME	☐ Petitioner ☐ Beneficiary	☐ Applicant
ADDRESS (Apt. No.) (Number & Street) (City)	(State)	(ZIP Code)

Check Applicable Item(s) below:

☐ 1. I am an attorney and a member in good standing of the bar of the Supreme Court of the United States or of the highest court of the following State, territory, insular possession, or District of Columbia

_____   _____ and am not under a
(Name of Court)

court or administrative agency order suspending, enjoining, restraining, disbarring, or otherwise restricting me in practicing law.

☐ 2. I am an accredited representative of the following named religious, charitable, social service, or similar organization established in the United States and which is so recognized by the Board:

☐ 3. I am associated with _____
the attorney of record who previously filed a notice of appearance in this case and my appearance is at his request. *(If you check this item, also check item 1 or 2 whichever is appropriate.)*

☐ 4. Others (Explain fully.)

SIGNATURE	COMPLETE ADDRESS
NAME (Type or Print)	TELEPHONE NUMBER

PURSUANT TO THE PRIVACY ACT OF 1974, I HEREBY CONSENT TO THE DISCLOSURE TO THE FOLLOWING NAMED ATTORNEY OR REPRESENTATIVE OF ANY RECORD PERTAINING TO ME WHICH APPEARS IN ANY IMMIGRATION AND NATURALIZATION SERVICE SYSTEM OF RECORDS: _____
(Name of Attorney or Representative)

THE ABOVE CONSENT TO DISCLOSE IS IN CONNECTION WITH THE FOLLOWING MATTER:

NAME OF PERSON CONSENTING	SIGNATURE OF PERSON CONSENTING	DATE

(NOTE: Execution of this box is required under the Privacy Act of 1974 where the person being represented is a citizen of the United States or an alien lawfully admitted for permanent residence.)

Form G - 28
(Rev. 10-25-79)N

(OVER)

UNITED STATES DEPARTMENT OF JUSTICE
Immigration and Naturalization Service

Stock Number 027-002-00218-1

For sale by the Superintendent of Documents, U.S. Government Printing Office, Washington, D.C. 20402

G28 ID Number _____

1. Form allowing attorney to represent client.

U.S. Department of Justice
Immigration and Naturalization Service

OMB No. 1115-0168
Petition for a Nonimmigrant Worker

START HERE - Please Type or Print

Part 1.   Information about the employer filing this petition.
If the employer is an individual, use the top name line. Organizations
should use the second line.

Family Name	Given Name	Middle Initial

Company or Organization Name

Address - Attn:

Street Number and Name		Apt. #
City	State or Province	
Country	Zip/Postal Code	

IRS Tax #

Part 2.   Information about this Petition.
(See instructions to determine the fee)

1. **Requested Nonimmigrant classification:**
   (write classification symbol at right)
2. **Basis for Classification** (check one)
   a. ☐ New employment
   b. ☐ Continuation of previously approved employment without change
   c. ☐ Change in previously approved employment
   d. ☐ New concurrent employment
3. **Prior Petition.** If you checked other than "New Employment" in item 2 (above) give the most recent prior petition numbers for the worker(s):
4. **Requested Action:** (check one)
   a. ☐ Notify the office in Part 4 so the person(s) can obtain a visa or be admitted (NOTE: a petition is not required for an E-1, E-2, or R visa)
   b. ☐ Change the person(s) status and extend their stay since they are all now in the U.S. in another status (see instructions for limitations). This is available only where you check "New Employment" in item 2, above.
   c. ☐ Extend or amend the stay of the person(s) since they now hold this status.
5. **Total number of workers in petition:**

   (See instructions for where more than one worker can be included)

Part 3.   Information about the person(s) you are filing for.
Complete the blocks below. Use the continuation sheet to name each person included in this petition.

If an entertainment group, give their group name.

Family Name	Given Name	Middle Initial
Date of Birth (Month/Day/Year)	Country of Birth	
Social Security #	A #	

If in the United States, complete the following:

Date of Arrival (Month/Day/Year)	I-94 #
Current Nonimmigrant Status	Expires (Month/Day/Year)

Form I-129 (Rev. 12/11/91)N   *Continued on back.*

FOR INS USE ONLY

Returned	Receipt
Resubmitted	
Reloc Sent	
Reloc Rec'd	

Interviewed
☐ Petitioner
☐ Beneficiary

Class: _____
# of Workers: _____
Priority Number: _____
Validity Dates: From _____
To _____

☐ **Classification Approved**
  ☐ Consulate/POE/PFI Notified
  At: _____
  ☐ Extension Granted
  ☐ COS/Extension Granted
Partial Approval (explain)

Action Block

To be Completed by Attorney or Representative, if any
☐ Fill in box if G-28 is attached to represent the applicant
VOLAG#

ATTY State License #

2. For non-immigrant work visas

Part 4. Processing Information

a. If the person named in Part 3 is outside the U.S. or a requested extension of stay or change of status cannot be granted, give the U.S. consulate or inspection facility you want to be notified if this petition is approved.

Type of Office (check one): ☐ Consulate	☐ Pre-flight inspection	☐ Port of Entry
Office Address (City)		U.S. State or Foreign Country
Person's Foreign Address		

b. Does each person in this petition have a valid passport?

☐ Not required to have passport ☐ No - explain on separate paper ☐ Yes

c. Are you filing any other petitions with this one? ☐ No ☐ Yes - How many? _____

d. Are applications for replacement/initial I-94's being filed with this petition? ☐ No ☐ Yes - How many? _____

e. Are applications by dependents being filed with this petition? ☐ No ☐ Yes - How many? _____

f. Is any person in this petition in exclusion or deportation proceedings? ☐ No ☐ Yes - explain on separate paper

g. Have you ever filed an immigrant petition for any person in this petition? ☐ No ☐ Yes - explain on separate paper

h. If you indicated you were filing a new petition in Part 2, within the past seven years has any person in this petition:

1) ever been given the classification you are now requesting? ☐ No ☐ Yes - explain on separate paper

2) ever been denied the classification you are now requesting? ☐ No ☐ Yes - explain on separate paper

i. If you are filing for an entertainment group, has any person in this petition not been with the group for at least 1 year?

☐ No ☐ Yes - explain on separate paper

Part 5. Basic Information about the proposed employment and employer.

Attach the supplement relating to the classification you are requesting.

Job Title	Nontechnical Description of Job

Address where the person(s) will work if different from the address in Part 1.

Is this a full-time position?		Wages per week or per year
☐ No - Hours per week	☐ Yes	
Other Compensation (Explain)	Value per week or per year	Dates of intended employment From: To:
Type of petitioner - check one ☐ U.S. citizen or permanent resident	☐ Organization	☐ Other - explain on separate paper
Type of business		Year established
Current number of employees	Gross Annual Income	Net Annual Income

Part 6. Signature.

Read the information on penalties in the instructions before completing this section.

I certify, under penalty of perjury under the laws of the United States of America, that this petition, and the evidence submitted with it, is all true and correct. If filing this on behalf of an organization, I certify that I am empowered to do so by that organization. If this petition is to extend a prior petition, I certify that the proposed employment is under the same terms and conditions as in the prior approved petition. I authorize the release of any information from my records, or from petitioning organization's records, which the Immigration and Naturalization Service needs to determine eligibility for the benefit being sought.

Signature and title	Print Name	Date

Please note: If you do not completely fill out this form and the required supplement, or fail to submit required documents listed in the instructions, then the person(s) filed for may not be found eligible for the requested benefit, and this petition may be denied.

Part 7. Signature of person preparing form if other than above.

I declare that I prepared this application at the request of the above person and it is based on all information of which I have knowledge.

Signature	Print Name	Date

Firm Name and Address

OMB No. 1115-0168
E Classification

U.S. Department of Justice
Immigration and Naturalization Service

Supplement to Form I-129

Name of person or organization filing petition:	Name of person you are filing for:

Classification sought (check one):	Name of country signatory to treaty with U.S.
☐ E-1 Treaty trader ☐ E-2 Treaty Investor	

Section 1. Information about the Employer outside the U.S. (if any)

Name	Address
Alien's Position - Title, duties and number of years employed	Principal Product, merchandise or service
Total number of Employees	

Section 2. Additional Information about the U.S. Employer.

The U.S. company is, to the company outside the U.S. (check one):
☐ Parent ☐ Branch ☐ Subsidiary ☐ Affiliate ☐ Joint Venture

Date and Place of Incorporation or establishment in the U.S.

Nationality of Ownership (Individual or Corporate)

Name	Nationality	Immigration Status	% Ownership

Assets	Net Worth	Total Annual Income

Staff in the U.S.	Executive/Manager	Specialized Qualifications or Knowledge
Nationals of Treaty Country in E or L Status		
Total number of employees in the U.S.		

Total number of employees the alien would supervise; or describe the nature of specialized skills essential to the U.S. company.

Section 3. Complete if filing for an E-1 Treaty Trader

Total Annual Gross Trade/Business of the U.S. company   For Year Ending

$

Percent of total gross trade which is between the U.S. and the country of which the treaty trader organization is a national.

Section 4. Complete if filing for an E-2 Treaty Investor

Total Investment	Cash	Equipment	Other
	$	$	$
	Inventory	Premises	Total
	$	$	$

3. Supplement for E visa

OMB No. 1115-0168

U.S. Department of Justice
Immigration and Naturalization Service

H Classification
Supplement to Form I-129

Name of person or organization filing petition:

Name of person or total number of workers you are filing for:

List the alien's and any dependent family members' prior periods of stay in H classification in the U.S. for the last six years. Be sure to list only those periods in which the alien and/or family members were actually in the U.S. in an H classification. If more space is needed, attach an additional sheet.

Classification sought (check one):

- [ ] H-1A   Registered Professional nurse
- [ ] H-1B1   Specialty occupation
- [ ] H-1B2   Exceptional services relating to a cooperative research and development project administered by the U.S. Department of Defense
- [ ] H-1B3   Artist, entertainer or fashion model of national or international acclaim

- [ ] H-1B4   Artist or entertainer in unique or traditional art form
- [ ] H-1B5   Athlete
- [ ] H-1BS   Essential support personnel for H-1B entertainer or athlete
- [ ] H-2A   Agricultural worker
- [ ] H-2B   Nonagricultural worker
- [ ] H-3   Trainee
- [ ] H-3   Special education exchange visitor program

Section 1.   Complete this section if filing for H-1A or H1B classification.

Describe the proposed duties

Alien's present occupation and summary of prior work experience

Statement for H-1B specialty occupations only:

By filing this petition, I agree to the terms of the labor condition application for the duration of the alien's authorized period of stay for H1-B employment

Petitioner's Signature   Date

Statement for H-1B specialty occupations and DOD projects:

As an authorized official of the employer, I certify that the employer will be liable for the reasonable costs of the return transportation of the alien abroad if the alien is dismissed from employment by the employer before the end of the period of the authorized stay.

Signature of authorized official of employer   Date

Statement for H1-B DOD projects only:

I certify that the alien will be working on a cooperative research and development project under a reciprocal Government-to-Government agreement administered by the Department of Defense.

DOD project manager's signature   Date

Section 2.   Complete this section if filing for H-2A or H-2B classification.

Employment is: (check one)		Temporary need is: (check one)	
[ ] Seasonal		[ ] Unpredictable	
[ ] Peakload		[ ] Periodic	
[ ] Intermittent		[ ] Recurrent Annually	
[ ] One-time occurrence			

Explain your temporary need for alien's services (attach a separate paper if additional space is needed).

Form I-129 Supplement H (12/11/91) N   *Continued on back.*

4. Supplement for H visa

OMB No. 1115-0168

U.S. Department of Justice
Immigration and Naturalization Service

L Classification
Supplement to Form I-129

Name of person or organization filing petition: Name of person you are filing for:

This petition is (check one):   ☐ An individual petition   ☐ A blanket petition

Section 1.   Complete this section if filing an individual petition

Classification (check one):   ☐ L-1A manager or executive   ☐ L-1B specialized knowledge

List the alien's, and any dependent family members' prior periods of stay in an L classification in the U.S. for the last seven years. Be sure to list only those periods in which the alien and/or family members were actually in the U.S. in an L classification.

Name and address of employer abroad

Dates of alien's employment with this employer. Explain any interruptions in employment.

Description of alien's duties for the past three years.

Description of alien's proposed duties in the U.S.

Summarize the alien's education and work experience.

The U.S. company is, to the company abroad: (check one)
☐ Parent   ☐ Branch   ☐ Subsidiary   ☐ Affiliate   ☐ Joint Venture

Describe the stock ownership and managerial control of each company.

Do the companies currently have the same qualifying relationship as they did during the one-year period of the alien's employment with the company abroad   ☐ Yes   ☐ No (attach explanation)

Is the alien coming to the U.S. to open a new office?
☐ Yes (explain in detail on separate paper)   ☐ No

Section 2.   Complete this section if filing a blanket petition.

List all U.S. and foreign parent, branches, subsidiaries and affiliates included in this petition.(Attach separate paper if additional space is needed)

Name and Address   Relationship

Explain in detail on separate paper.

Form I-129 Supplement E/L (12/11/91)N

5. Supplement for L visa

U.S. Department of Justice
Immigration and Naturalization Service

OMB #1115-006
Immigrant Petition for Alien Worker

START HERE - Please Type or Print	FOR INS USE ONLY

Part 1. Information about person or organization filing this petition.

If an individual is filing, use the top Name line. Organizations should use the second line.

Family Name	Given Name	Middle Initial

Company or Organization

Address - Attn:

Street Number and Name		Room #

City	State or Province	

Country	ZIP/Postal Code

IRS Tax #	Social Security #

FOR INS USE ONLY

Returned

Receipt

Resubmitted

Reloc Sent

Reloc Rec'd

☐ Petitioner Interviewed
☐ Beneficiary Interviewed

Classification
☐ 203(b)(1)(A) Alien of Extraordinary Ability
☐ 203(b)(1)(B) Outstanding Professor or Researcher
☐ 203(b)(1)(C) Multi-national executive or manager
☐ 203(b)(2) Member of professions w/adv degree or of exceptional ability
☐ 203(b)(3)(A)(i) Skilled worker
☐ 203(b)(3)(A)(ii) Professional
☐ 203(b)(3)(A)(iii) Other worker
☐ Sec. 124 IMMACT-Employee of U.S. business in Hong Kong

Priority Date	Consulate

Remarks

Action Block

Part 2. Petition Type. This petition is being filed for: (check one)

a. ☐ An alien of extraordinary ability
b. ☐ An outstanding professor or researcher
c. ☐ A multinational executive or manager
d. ☐ A member of the professions holding an advanced degree or an alien of exceptional ability
e. ☐ A skilled worker (requiring at least two years of specialized training or experience) or professional
f. ☐ An employee of a U.S. business operating in Hong Kong
g. ☐ Any other worker (requiring less than two years training or experience)

Part 3. Information about the person this petition is for.

Family Name	Given Name	Middle Initial

Address - C/O

Street Number and Name		Apt. #

City	State or Province	

Country	ZIP/Postal Code

Date of Birth (Month/Day/Year)	Country of Birth

Social Security # (if any)	A # (if any)

if in the U.S.	Date of Arrival ((Month/Day/Year)	I-94#
	Current Nonimmigrant Status	Expires on (Month/Day/Year)

Part 4. Processing Information.

Below give the U.S. Consulate you want notified if this petition is approved and if any requested adjustment of status cannot be granted.

U.S. Consulate: City	Country

Form I-140 (Rev. 12-2-91)   *Continued on back.*

To Be Completed by
Attorney or Representative, if any

■ Fill in box if G-28 is attached to represent the applicant

VOLAG#

ATTY State License #

6. For employment based green cards

Part 4. Processing Information. *(continued)*

If you gave a U.S. address in Part 3, print the person's foreign address below. If his/her native alphabet does not use Roman letters, print his/her name and foreign address in the native alphabet.

Name   Address

	No	yes attach an explanation
Are you filing any other petitions or applications with this one?	☐ No	☐ yes attach an explanation
Is the person you are filing for in exclusion or deportation proceedings?	☐ No	☐ yes attach an explanation
Has an immigrant visa petition ever been filed by or in behalf of this person?	☐ No	☐ yes attach an explanation

Part 5. Additional information about the employer.

Type of petitioner (check one)	☐ Self	☐ Individual U.S. Citizen	☐ Company or organization
	☐ Permanent Resident	☐ Other explain _____	

If a company, give the following:
Type of business

Date established	Current # of employees	Gross Annual Income	Net Annual Income
If an individual, give the following: Occupation		Annual Income	

Part 6. Basic information about the proposed employment.

Job Title	Nontechnical description of job

Address where the person will work
if different from address in Part 1.

Is this a full-time position?	☐ yes	☐ No (hours per week _____)	Wages per week
Is this a permanent position?	☐ yes ☐ No	Is this a new position? ☐ yes ☐ No	

Part 7. Information on spouse and all children of the person you are filing for.

Provide an attachment listing the family members of the person you are filing for. Be sure to include their full name, relationship, date and country of birth. and present address.

Part 8. Signature. *Read the information on penalties in the instructions before completing this section.*

I certify under penalty of perjury under the laws of the United States of America that this petition, and the evidence submitted with it, is all true and correct. I authorize the release of any information from my records which the Immigration and Naturalization Service needs to determine eligibility for the benefit I am seeking.

Signature   Date

Please Note: If you do not completely fill out this form, or fail to submit required documents listed in the instructions, you cannot be found eligible for the requested document and this application may be denied.

Part 9. Signature of person preparing form if other than above. *(Sign below)*

I declare that I prepared this application at the request of the above person and it is based on all information of which I have knowledge.

Signature   Print Your Name   Date

Firm Name
and Address

U.S. Department of Justice
Immigration and Naturalization Service

OMB #1115-0093
Application to Extend/ChangeNonimmigrant Status

START HERE - Please Type or Print

Part 1. Information about you.

Family Name	Given Name	Middle Initial

Address - In Care of:

Street # and Name		Apt. #

City	State	

Zip Code

Date of Birth (month/day/year)	Country of Birth
Social Security # (if any)	A # (if any)
Date of Last Arrival Into the U.S.	I-94#
Current Nonimmigrant Status	Expires on (month/day/year)

Part 2. Application Type.   (See Instructions for fee.)

1. I am applying for: (check one)
   a. ☐ an extension of stay in my current status
   b. ☐ a change of status. The new status I am requesting is: _____

2. Number of people included in this application: (check one)
   a. ☐ I am the only applicant
   b. ☐ Members of my family are filing this application with me.
   The Total number of people included in this application is _____
   (complete the supplement for each co-applicant)

Part 3. Processing information.

1. I/We request that my/our current or requested status be extended until (month/day/year) _____

2. Is this application based on an extension or change of status already granted to your spouse, child or parent?
   ☐ No   ☐ Yes (receipt # _____)

3. Is this application being filed based on a separate petition or application to give your spouse, child or parent an extension or change of status?
   ☐ No   ☐ Yes, filed with this application ☐ Yes, filed previously and pending with INS

4. If you answered yes to question 3, give the petitioner or applicant name:

   _____

   If the application is pending with INS, also give the following information.

Office filed at _____	Filed on _____	(date)

Part 4. Additional information.

1. For applicant # 1, provide passport information:
Country of issuance	Valid to: (month/day/year)

2. Foreign address:
Street # and Name		Apt#
City or Town	State or Province	
Country	Zip or Postal Code	

Form I-539 (Rev. 12-2-91)   *Continued on back.*

FOR INS USE ONLY

Returned	Receipt
Date	
Resubmitted	
Date	
Reloc Sent	
Date	
Reloc Rec'd	
Date	

☐ Applicant Interviewed

☐ *Extension Granted*
   to (date):_____

☐ *Change of Status/Extension Granted*
New Class:_____ To (date):_____

If denied:
☐ Still within period of stay

☐ V/D to: _____

☐ S/D to:_____

☐ Place under docket control

Remarks

Action Block

To Be Completed by
Attorney or *Representative*, if any
■ Fill in box if G-28 is attached to represent the applicant

VOLAG#

ATTY State License #

7. Extend or change stay status in US

Part 4.   Additional information. *(continued)*

3. Answer the following questions. If you answer yes to any question, explain on separate paper.	Yes	No
a. Are you, or any other person included in this application, an applicant for an immigrant visa or adjustment of status to permanent residence?		
b. Has an immigrant petition ever been filed for you, or for any other person included in this application?		
c. Have you, or any other person included in this application ever been arrested or convicted of any criminal offense since last entering the U.S.?		
d. Have you, or any other person included in this application done anything which violated the terms of the nonimmigrant status you now hold?		
e. Are you, or any other person included in this application, now in exclusion or deportation proceedings?		
f. Have you, or any other person included in this application, been employed in the U.S. since last admitted or granted an extension or change of status?		

If you answered YES to question 3f, give the following information on a separate paper: Name of person, name of employer, address of employer, weekly income, and whether specifically authorized by INS.

If you answered NO to question 3f, fully describe how you are supporting yourself on a separate paper. Include the source and the amount and basis for any income.

Part 5.   Signature. *Read the information on penalties in the instructions before completing this section. You must file this application while in the United States.*

I certify under penalty of perjury under the laws of the United States of America that this application, and the evidence submitted with it, is all true and correct. I authorize the release of any information from my records which the Immigration and Naturalization Service needs to determine eligibility for the benefit I am seeking.

Signature   Print your name   Date

Please Note: If you do not completely fill out this form, or fail to submit required documents listed in the instructions, you cannot be found eligible for the requested document and this application will have to be denied.

Part 6.   Signature of person preparing form if other than above. *(Sign below)*

I declare that I prepared this application at the request of the above person and it is based on all information of which I have knowledge.

Signature   Print Your Name   Date

Firm Name
and Address

(Please remember to enclose the mailing label with your application)

OMB Approval No. 44-R1301

U.S. DEPARTMENT OF LABOR
Employment and Training Administration

APPLICATION
FOR
ALIEN EMPLOYMENT CERTIFICATION

IMPORTANT: READ CAREFULLY BEFORE COMPLETING THIS FORM
PRINT legibly in ink or use typewriter. If you need more space to answer questions on this form, use a separate sheet. Identify each answer with the number of the corresponding question. SIGN AND DATE each sheet in original signature.

To knowingly furnish any false information in the preparation of this form and any supplement thereto or aid, abet, or counsel another to do so is a felony punishable by $10,000 fine or 5 years in the penitentiary, or both (18 U.S.C. 1001).

PART A. OFFER OF EMPLOYMENT

1. Name of Alien   *(Family name in capital letter, First, Middle, Maiden)*

2. Present Address of Alien   *(Number, Street, City, State ZIP Code, or Province, Country)*

3. Type of Visa   *(If in U.S.)*

The following information is submitted as evidence of an offer of employment.

4. Name of Employer   *(Full name of organization)*

5. Telephone   *(Area Code and Number)*

6. Address   *(Number, Street, City, State, Zip, Country)*

7. Address Where Alien Will Work   *(If different from Item 6)*

8. Nature of Employer's Business Activity	9. Name of Job Title	10. Total Hours Per Week		11. Work Schedule (Hourly)	12. Rate of Pay	
		a. Basic	b. Overtime	a.m. p.m.	a. Basic $ per	b. Overtime $ per hour

13. Describe fully the Job to be Performed

14. State in detail the MINIMUM education, training, and experience for a worker to perform satisfactorily the job duties described in Item 13 above.

15. Other Special Requirements

EDU-CATION *(Enter number of years)*	Grade School	High School	College	College Degree Required *(specify)*
				Major Field of Study

TRAIN-ING	No. Yrs.	No. Mos.	Type of Training

EXPERI-ENCE	Job Offered		Related Occupation	Related Occupation *(specify)*
	Yrs.	Mos.	Number Yrs. Mos.	

16. Occupational Title of Person Who Will Be Alien's Immediate Supervisor   -> ->

17. Number of Employees Alien will Supervise   -> 0

<-- ENDORSEMENTS   *(Make no entry in section - for government use only)*

Date Forms Received	
L.O.	S.O.
R.O.	N.O.
Ind. Code	Occ. Code
Occ. Title	

Replaces MA 7-50A, B, and C (Apr. 1970 edition) which is obsolete.

ETA 750 (Oct 1979)

8. For labor certification

18. COMPLETE ITEMS ONLY IF JOB IS TEMPORARY			19. IF JOB IS UNIONIZED (Complete)	
a. No. of Open-ings To Be Filled By Aliens Under Job Offer	b. Exact Dates You Expect To Employ Alien		a. Number of Local	b. Name of Local
	From	**To**		
				c. City and State

20. STATEMENT FOR LIVE-AT-WORK JOB OFFERS   (Complete for Private Household Job ONLY)

a. Description of Residence		b. No Persons Residing at Place of Employment				c. Will free board and private room not shared with any-one be provided?	(*"X" one*)
(*"X" one*)	Number of Rooms	Adults		Children	Ages		☐ Yes ☐ No
☐ House			BOYS				
☐ Apartment			GIRLS				

21. DESCRIBE EFFORTS TO RECRUIT U.S. WORKERS AND THE RESULTS.   (Specify Sources of Recruitment by Name)

22. Applications require various types of documentation. Please read Part II of the instructions to assure that appropriate supporting documentation is included with your application.

23. EMPLOYER CERTIFICATIONS

By virtue of my signature below, I HEREBY CERTIFY the following conditions of employment.

a. I have enough funds available to pay the wage or salary offered the alien.

b. The wage offered equals or exceeds the pre-vailing wage and I guarantee that, if a labor certi-fication is granted, the wage paid to the alien when the alien begins work will equal or exceed the pre-vailing wage which is applicable at the time the alien begins work.

c. The wage offered is not based on commissions, bonuses, or other incentives, unless I guarantee a wage paid on a weekly, bi-weekly, or monthly basis

d. I will be able to place the alien on the payroll on or before the date of the alien's proposed entrance into the United States.

e. The job opportunity does not involve unlawful discri-mination by race, creed, color, national origin, age, sex, religion, handicap, or citizenship.

f. The job opportunity is not:

(1) Vacant because the former occupant is on strike or is being locked out in the course of a labor dispute involving a work stoppage.

(2) At issue in a labor dispute involving a work stoppage.

g. The job opportunity's terms, conditions and occupa-tional environment are not contrary to Federal State or local law.

h. The job opportunity has been and is clearly open to any qualified U. S. worker.

24. DECLARATIONS

DECLARATION OF EMPLOYER -->	Pursuant to 28 U.S.C. 1746, I declare under penalty of perjury the foregoing is true and correct.	
SIGNATURE		DATE
NAME (Type or Print)	TITLE	

AUTHORIZATION OF AGENT OF EMPLOYER -->	I HEREBY DESIGNATE the agent below to represent me for the purpose of labor certification and I TAKE FULL RESPONSIBILTY for accuracy of any representations made by my agent.	
SIGNATURE OF EMPLOYER		DATE
NAME OF AGENT (Type or Print)	ADDRESS OF AGENT (Number, Street, City, State, ZIP Code)	

PART B. STATEMENT OF QUALIFICATIONS OF ALIEN

FOR ADVICE CONCERNING REQUIREMENTS FOR ALIEN EMPLOYMENT CERTIFICATION: *If alien is in the U.S., contact nearest office of*

Immigration and Naturalization Service. If alien is outside U.S., contact nearest U.S. Consulate.
IMPORTANT: READ ATTACHED INSTRUCTIONS BEFORE COMPLETING THIS FORM.
Print legibly in ink or use typewriter. If you need more space to fully answer any questions on this form, use a seperate sheet. Identify each answer with the number of the corresponding question. Sign and date each sheet.

1. Name of Alien *(Family name in capital letters)*	First name	Middle name	Maiden name

2. Present Address *(No., Street, City or Town, State or Province and ZIP Code*	Country	3. Type of Visa *(If in U.S.)*

4. Alien's Birthdate *(Month, Day, Year)*	5. Birthplace *(City or Town, State or Province)*	Country	6. Present Nationality or Citizenship *(Country)*

7. Address in United States Where Alien Will Reside

8. Name and Address of Prospective Employer if Alien has a job offer in U.S.	9. Occupation in which Alien is Seeking Work

10. "X" the appropriate box below and furnish the information required for the box marked

a. ☐ Alien will apply for a visa abroad at the American Consulate in _____ >   City in Foreign Country   Foreign Country

b. ☐ Alien is in the United States and will apply for adjustment of status to that of a lawful permanent resident in the office of the Immigration and Naturalization Service at _____ >   City   State

11. Names and Addresses of Schools, Colleges and Universities Attended *(Include trade or vocational training facilities)*	Field of Study	FROM		TO		Degrees or Certificates Received
		Month	Year	Month	Year	

SPECIAL QUALIFICATIONS AND SKILLS

12. Additional Qualifications and Skills Alien Possesses and Proficiency in the use of Tools, Machines or Equipment Which Would Help Establish if Alien Meets Requirements for Occupation in Item 9.

13. List Licenses   *(Professional, journeyman, etc.)*

14. List Documents Attached Which are Submitted as Evidence that Alien Possesses the Education, Training, Experience, and Abilities Represented

Endorsements	DATE REC. DOL
	O.T. & C.
(Make no entry in this section - FOR Government Agency USE ONLY)	

(Items continued on next page)

15. WORK EXPERIENCE. *List all jobs held during past three (3) years. Also, list any other jobs related to the occupation for which the alien is seeking certification as indicated in item 9.*

a. NAME AND ADDRESS OF EMPLOYER

NAME OF JOB	DATE STARTED		DATE LEFT		KIND OF BUSINESS
	Month	Year	Month	Year	

DESCRIBE IN DETAILS THE DUTIES PERFORMED, INCLUDING THE USE OF TOOLS, MACHINES, OR EQUIPMENT	NO. OF HOURS PER WEEK

b. NAME AND ADDRESS OF EMPLOYER

NAME OF JOB	DATE STARTED		DATE LEFT		KIND OF BUSINESS
	Month	Year	Month	Year	

DESCRIBE IN DETAILS THE DUTIES PERFORMED, INCLUDING THE USE OF TOOLS, MACHINES, OR EQUIPMENT	NO. OF HOURS PER WEEK

c. NAME AND ADDRESS OF EMPLOYER

NAME OF JOB	DATE STARTED		DATE LEFT		KIND OF BUSINESS
	Month	Year	Month	Year	

DESCRIBE IN DETAILS THE DUTIES PERFORMED, INCLUDING THE USE OF TOOLS, MACHINES, OR EQUIPMENT	NO. OF HOURS PER WEEK

16. DECLARATIONS

DECLARATION OF ALIEN ——> *Pursuant to 28 U.S.C. 1746, I declare under penalty of perjury the foregoing is true and correct.*

SIGNATURE OF ALIEN	DATE

AUTHORIZATION OF AGENT OF ALIEN ——> *I hereby designate the agent below to represent me for the purposes of labor certification and take full responsibly for accuracy of any representations made by my agent.*

SIGNATURE OF ALIEN	DATE

NAME OF AGENT (Type or print)	ADDRESS OF AGENT (No., Street, City, State, ZIP Code)

U.S. Department of Justice

Immigration and Naturalization Service

OMB #1115-0214

Affidavit of Support Under Section 213A of the Act

START HERE - Please Type or Print

Part 1. Information on Sponsor (You)

Last Name	First Name	Middle Name

Mailing Address (Street Number and Name)		Apt/Suite Number

City	State or Province

Country	ZIP/Postal Code	Telephone Number ( )

Place of Residence if different from above(Street Number and Name)	Apt/Suite Number

FOR AGENCY USE ONLY

City	State or Province

This Affidavit   Receipt

[ ] Meets

Country	ZIP/Postal Code	Telephone Number ( )

[ ] Does not meet

Date of Birth (Month, Day, Year)	Place of Birth (City, State, Country)	Are you a U.S. Citizen? ☐ Yes ☐ No

Requirements of Section 213A

Social Security Number	A-Number (If any)

Part 2. Basis for Filing Affidavit of Support

I am filing this affidavit of support because (check one):

a. ☐ I filed/am filing the alien relative petition.

b. ☐ I filed/am filing an alien worker petition on behalf of the intending immigrant, who is related to me as my _____.
(relationship)

c. ☐ I have ownership interest of at least 5% of _____,
(name of entity which filed visa petition)
which filed an alien worker petition on behalf of the intending immigrant, who is related to me as my _____.
(relationship)

d. ☐ I am a joint sponsor willing to accept the legal obligations with any other sponsor(s).

Officer's Signature

Location

Date

Part 3. Information on the Immigrant(s) You Are Sponsoring

Last Name	First Name	Middle Name

Date of Birth (Month,Day,Year)	Sex: ☐ Male ☐ Female	Social Security Number (If any)

Country of Citizenship	A-Number (If any)

Current Address (Street Number and Name)	Apt/Suite Number	City

State/Province	Country	ZIP/Postal Code	Telephone Number ( )

List any spouse and/or children immigrating with the immigrant named above in this Part: (Use additional sheet of paper if necessary.)

Name	Relationship to Sponsored Immigrant			Date of Birth			A-Number (If any)	Social Security Number (If any)
	Spouse	Son	Daughter	Mo.	Day	Yr.		

Form I-864 (10/6/97)

9. To prove financial support

U.S. Department of Justice
Immigration and Naturalization Service

Notice of Action

THE UNITED STATES OF AMERICA

RECEIPT NUMBER		CASE TYPE	
RECEIPT DATE August 21, 1996	**PRIORITY DATE** August 20, 1996	**APPLICANT**	
NOTICE DATE September 23, 1996	**PAGE** 1 of 1		

HENRY LIEBMAN
COE NORDWALL & LIEBMAN LLP
720 OLIVE WAY STE 1300
SEATTLE WA 98101

Notice Type: Approval Notice
Class: UNKNOWN

The above petition has been approved.

We have sent it to the **Department of State National Visa Center (NVC), 32 Rochester Avenue, Portsmouth, NH 03801-2909.** NVC processes all approved immigrant visa petitions that need consular action and also determines which consular post is the appropriate consulate to complete visa processing. The NVC will then forward the approved petition to that consulate.

This completes all INS action on this petition. If you have any questions about visa issuance, please contact the NVC directly. The telephone number to NVC is **(603) 334-0700.**

The NVC will contact the person for whom you are petitioning concerning further immigrant visa processing steps.

Please read the back of this form carefully for more information.

THIS FORM IS NOT A VISA NOR MAY IT BE USED IN PLACE OF A VISA.

Please see the additional information on the back. You will be notified separately about any other cases you filed.
NORTHERN SERVICE CENTER
U. S. IMMIG. & NATZ. SERVICE
P.O. BOX 82521
LINCOLN NE 68501-2521
Customer Service Telephone: 402-437-5218

10. Approval Notice

Glossary

Please refer to the glossary for answers to any questions about the specialised terms used in this book.

Adjustment of Status. The procedures for changing to permanent residence status through the INS.

Advance Parole. Permission to leave the US and re-enter during adjustment of status procedures.

Alien Registration Card. Formal name for green card.

Application for Immigrant Visa and Alien Registration. The procedures for applying for immigrant status through a consulate.

Arrival Departure Card. Issued at port of entry to evidence legal status.

Bilateral Investment Treaty, **Friendship Commerce** and **Navigation Treaties.** The agreements between the US and a foreign government which enable treaty trader or treaty investor status.

Change of Status. An application to the INS to change from one nonimmigrant status to another nonimmigrant status.

Consulates. Representative offices of a foreign country located in major cities of the host country. Consulates take care of trade, economic, political and visa issues.

Consuls. Foreign service employees who work in embassies and consulates. Consuls issue visas.

Department of State. The agency of the United States government responsible for managing its foreign affairs. This agency controls the issuing of visas for travel to the US.

Embassy. The representative office of a foreign country located in the capital city of the host country. Embassies take care of political, trade, economic and visa issues. An ambassator is the head of post at an embassy.

Essential Skill. A skill, essential to the success of the enterprise, that is generally unavailable in the US.

Executive. The person who establishes corporate goals and policies, and monitors the managers.

Extension of Stay. An application to the INS to extend the stay period listed on Form I-94.

Green Card. Common name for alien registration card for permanent residence.

I-94 Card. The form issued to temporary visitors to the US as evidence of their immigration status and allowed period of stay within the US.

Immigrant. A person who wants to live in the US for an indefinite period of time or permanently.

Immigration and Naturalization Service (INS). A sub-agency of the US Department of Justice responsible for controlling immigration within the US.

International organisation. A foreign and US company(ies) linked by 50 per cent or more common ownership.

Labor Certification. The process for determining that no US workers meet the offered job's minimum requirements. Unless exempted, labor certification is a prerequisite for employment-based green card categories.

Labor Conditions Application Process. A form filed with the Department of Labor for the purpose of notifying US workers that a foreign worker will be employed at the job site. Also used for the purpose of ensuring that the US employer is not hiring a foreign worker at less than the wages normally paid to US workers for the same position.

Manager. A person who manages other managers, supervisors or professionals within a business organisation. Managers implement corporate goals and policies through subordinates.

Multiple Entry Visa. Allows more than one entry into US.

Naturalization. The process for becoming a US citizen.

Nonimmigrant Status. A temporary status limited to a

particular purpose for a set period of time.

Petition. Generic name for the forms used by the INS to determine eligibility for various visa categories.

Preference system. System for allocating permanent residence visas by skills or family relationship.

Prevailing wage. The wage, determined by the Department of Labor, normally paid to US workers for a particular job.

Practical Training. A programme available to students that permits them to work in the US after or during university study.

Quota System. The system used to limit the number of visas available to each country for particular visa classifications.

Pilot Visa Waiver Program. An agreement with several countries and the US that permits each other's nationals to enter the country for business or pleasure purposes without a visa for up to 90 days.

Professionals. Persons with at least a four-year university degree, or equivalent in experience and education, in a recognised professional discipline such as accounting, law, engineering or the sciences.

Re-entry Permit. A declaration of one's intention to maintain US permanent residence during prolonged absences from the US.

Specialised knowledge. A narrowly-held skill which helps the US employer's ability to compete in international markets.

Treaty Investment. Substantial investment in the US made by treaty companies or individuals.

Treaty Trade. Substantial trade between the US and a foreign country.

Visa. Permission to apply for entry to a country, usually issued by a country's foreign service.

Visa Revalidation. An application to the Visa Office in Washington D.C. for a new visa of the same type.

Visa Waiver. Entry to US without a visa – certain countries qualify.

Index